5 WAY
MANAGEMENT

5 WAY MANAGEMENT

MAXIMISING YOUR ALL ROUND IMPACT

ANDREW FORREST

THE INDUSTRIAL SOCIETY
and
STIRLING USA

First published 1997 by
The Industrial Society
Robert Hyde House
48 Bryanston Square
London W1H 7LN

© The Industrial Society 1997

Stirling
22883 Quicksilver Drive
Stirling VA
USA

ISBN 1 85835 477 3

British Library Cataloguing-in-Publication Data.
A Catalogue record for this book is available from the
British Library.

Library of Congress
Cataloguing-in-Publication
Data on File

Typeset by: Midland Book Typesetting
Printed by: Lavenham Press
Cover Design: Rhodes Design

The Industrial Society is a Registered Charity No. 290003

5 WAY
MANAGEMENT

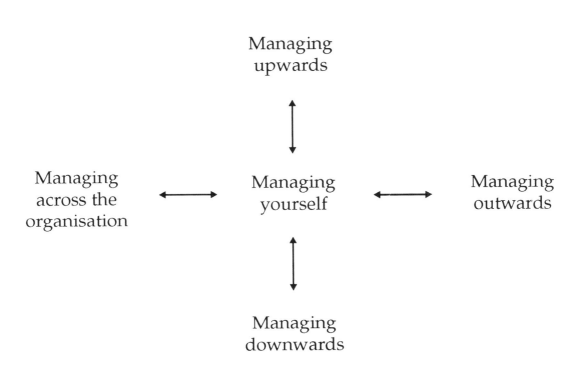

The 5 Way Management Model

acknowledgements

I am very grateful to:

- Jenny Clayton and VT Southern Careers Ltd for the grid depicting careers guidance in Hampshire (Appendix 3)
- Hutchinson Publishers for the extract from *A Soldier's Way* by Colin Powell
- Sue Lilley and Liz Friend of the Department for Education and Employment, and Mike Lewis of The Cabinet Office, for the Employment Service project described in Appendix 2
- Marie Mosely and the publishers of Maxim for *How to manage your boss* in Appendix 1
- Ordnance Survey for the extract from their annual report
- Post Office Counters for their account of how service level agreements operate
- PowerGen, 3M, Rover, Mercury One2One, The National Trust, Reebok, BICC, Ministry of Defence and Trifast for the examples of good practice mentioned in the text
- A group of managers who attended The Industrial Society's course *Management Skills for women* and put 5-way management into practice as a result
- My colleagues Mairi McBain (for research), Christine Curtiss and Susannah Rogers (for keyboard skills) and Sheridan Maguire of the Industrial Society, patience personified in a publisher.

Contents

introduction

This book is for managers who want to operate at their 'added value' level, where they are being most effective and most fulfilled.

The idea of 5-way management started from a review of the range of training available to managers. I was struck by the enormous number of courses dealing with how to manage your staff, how to organise yourself, and how to relate to colleagues. But there appeared to be a corresponding lack of training in how to manage upwards and how to deal with the huge variety of external influences on your organisation, beyond the obvious category of customers.

So the basic structure of 5-way management emerged as a way of filling these gaps: an inventory of training topics. But it soon became clear that the model was also relevant in viewing the manager's job in perspective. With time such a precious resource, how much of a manager's time should be spent on each of these five aspects? It is hard to generalise, but it is a healthy discipline for any manager to check whether he or she has the proportions right — and to check at intervals — to avoid becoming stuck in one of two ruts:

1   spending most time on what you have always done or
2   spending most time on what you most enjoy, even if that is not the most important part of the job.

Further applications of the model followed. At director level, managing upwards is by definition not applicable. It is replaced by 'overseeing the organisation', (see chapter six), which is not the same as managing downwards.

The 5-way model is an excellent basis for an integrated

communication structure, in which the relative merits of each method of communication are exploited. This is covered in chapter seven. Chapter eight deals with 360° appraisal, which has spread very quickly in various versions across British organisations over the last few years. 5-way management has much to offer if you want to use the 360° approach.

Throughout the book 'he' and 'she' have been used interchangeably. 5-way management is not the prerogative of one gender.

Your initial reaction may be that in this era of flatter structures and the obsolescence of hierarchy, 5-way management is an inappropriate model because it uses language such as 'managing downwards'. Not so: firstly because you do not have to act in a 'command and control' manner to approach your job with an all-round perspective. Secondly the traditional preoccupation of managers has been managing downwards, which has the strongest hierarchical connotations. The 5-way management approach draws long-overdue attention to the remaining four aspects. Many managers tell me that in a flatter structure, their relationship 'upwards' with their immediate manager has become more crucial than ever.

> **The purpose of 5-way management is to enable you to see your work in perspective, and thus ensure that you are delivering your own unique 'added value'. By doing so you optimise both your contribution to your organisation and your own job satisfaction: a win/win situation.**

1 managing yourself

Analyse Your Personal Contribution to the job

Every manager should be striving to build effective relationships upwards, downwards, outwards and across the organisation. But an equal if not greater priority is to manage yourself: to 'get your act together'. This includes being both fit and efficient, which we will deal with shortly. But there is not much point in being efficient at the wrong activities.

So your first opportunity to use 5-way management is to take stock of your personal contribution to the organisation — your added value. It is best to start this analysis yourself, and then to talk it through with a colleague. First, look at the contribution required from the role which you fill (independent of yourself as the person currently in the role). If you are the Customer Service Manager, why does that role exist? Or if you are a quality co-ordinator, why was the role created? Questions to ask yourself include:

- What is the special contribution of this role?
- What makes it different from other similar posts?
- How up to date is the job description?
- Does the job title accurately reflect the job's demands?
- Is the reality of the work significantly different from what it is supposed to be?
- How well understood is this job in the organisation?

Because it can be difficult to disentangle the job from yourself as the job holder, you may find it helpful to

3

discuss your responses with a colleague. This will apply particularly to the second stage of analysis, namely your personal contribution. You may have created the role from scratch, or inherited it from a not-very-competent predecessor, or taken over from a much respected manager. Whichever route brought you into the role, you will have made it your own in all sorts of obvious and less obvious ways. A dramatic example of this at top level came when George Simpson succeeded Lord Weinstock as chief executive of GEC. Lord Weinstock had led GEC for many years with a strong background in accountancy. When George Simpson took over, he was presented with a hefty pile of computer printouts of detailed financial reports from GEC's operating companies. He swept them aside with the comment, "That was the past: I am the future."

You are unlikely to have quite this buccaneering approach to your own work, but you should still be able to identify your individual style. Questions which may help you are:

- What were the main changes which I made when I took on this job?
- Which aspects of the job consume most of my time?
- What do I find most difficult in the job?
- What do I find enjoyable about the work?
- What do I find frustrating?
- Does the role use all of my skills? If not, which are getting rusty?
- How good are my relationships with colleagues, my team, my manager, and external contacts?
- What one piece of advice will I give to my successor when the time comes?

Once you have gone through the analysis, first of your job then of your personal contribution, you can use five-way management to consider whether there is a good match between the two. Under 'managing upwards', are you encroaching on your manager's role, e.g. by nibbling at responsibilities which are his or hers? If so this is not necessarily anything to be ashamed of — it may be that you can take on more responsibility, in which case you can open up that dialogue.

Under 'managing downwards', are you second-guessing what your team are doing? Are you breathing down their necks? Are you giving them enough scope — e.g. to let them do things their way, which may not be your way but can be equally effective?

Under 'managing outwards', are you taking a proactive stance, using your antennae to predict customers' requirements or regulators' demands? Or are you always on the defensive, responding to external influences?

Under 'managing across the organisation', is there overlap between yourself and any colleagues? Have you agreed mutual boundaries or do you carry out border raids on your colleagues' areas? So if the *actual* boundaries of your role (up, down outwards and across) are fluid rather than neat, this is not necessarily wrong. It may simply reflect reality: you have moulded the job to fit your skills.

But there are two other checks you need to make on the actual shape of your role:

1 Within your role are there any black holes — responsibilities which you are uncomfortable with and dislike, so that either they are never achieved or are tackled half-heartedly? We all have something of this kind: mine is budgeting. I am glad to delegate it rather than carry it out myself, but I remain accountable for fulfiling my budget commitments — they cannot be delegated.

2 (and even more productive) What skills do you personally possess which your role does not require? An obvious example would be if you can speak Spanish but the job description says nothing about foreign languages.

We each owe it to ourselves and to our employers to make these skills known, and see if they can be put to use within the work situation. After all they are what we are good at and enjoy, so why not deploy them?

A realistic and flexible approach to role definition

What I am advocating is a realistic and flexible approach to role definition. Of course the organisation needs to have its objectives achieved, but the days are surely past when that had to be by such tight definition of responsibilities that each person feels a prisoner in a box. Better to get into a negotiation with those whose roles are adjacent to your own, and adjust the boundaries so that everybody wins.

It is far from self-indulgent to identify and exploit our own unique blend of skills — it is in fact the best contribution we can offer our organisation. If you are one of team of design engineers but you happen to be brilliant at chairing meetings, your company may well benefit most if you spend three-quarters of your time chairing meetings (or any subject) and simply 'keep your hand in' with some design work. Most organisations would pay a king's ransom for someone skilled at chairing meetings, because the cost of poor chairmanship is so great.

Whilst we as managers can let rip ourselves in this way, drafting our own job descriptions, we owe it to all employees to look out for talent beyond the confines of their job. The housekeeper of a major hotel told me that she keeps an inventory of all the foreign languages which her staff can speak. One of the chambermaids speaks Polish, and when any Polish guests arrive, the chambermaid introduces herself and offers any help as an interpreter. In similar fashion, what skills are lurking among your staff?

Time management

If you have gone to all the trouble of identifying your own added value, it stands to reason that you should aim to operate at your added value level for as much of the working week as possible. You do not need an MBA degree to know that the top three causes of failure to do this are telephone interruptions, paper shuffling, and what is best called 'self-indulgent dabbling'. Any number of books on time management supply techniques for dealing with the first two of these. To eradicate the third requires a greater effort of will. 'Self-indulgent dabbling' means dipping in and out of the part of your role which you most enjoy, but which is often not the most important aspect. Confessional starts here: I am tempted to spend time scanning business newspapers and magazines for interesting items which I then cut out and inflict on my colleagues. I genuinely believe this is useful to them, but I need to ration how much time I spend on it.

A more damaging type of self-indulgent dabbling is where you cannot quite let go of the previous post which you held, and you continue to meddle in it. If this post is in someone else's department your meddling will not be tolerated for long. But if you have been promoted from within your own team, you may be looking over the shoulder of your successor in that role and restricting her headroom. The best cure is to apply the added value principle — for you to operate at your added value level you must allow everyone else to operate at theirs. "Don't crowd me!"

One of the main purposes of 5-way management is that it enables you to make regular checks on whether you have divided your time in roughly the right proportions between the five areas. This does *not* mean exactly 20% on each; it means being proactive, making sure that the proportions are as you wish them to be and not as a result of you being disorganised. For instance many managers acknowledge that they should be out and about much more, but are either deskbound by paperwork or forever closeted in internal meetings.

> **5-way management provides a route to alter the proportions in the way that you wish. The**

> 'managing yourself' area acts rather like a junction box.

Take the example above: you are bogged down by internal meetings and want to get away from the office to visit suppliers. Rather than make New Year resolutions about it which collapse by mid-March, set yourself a measurable change, e.g. to cut half a day a week from meetings (managing across) and transfer that time to supplier visits (managing outwards).

To achieve this switch your route takes you through 'managing yourself' where you ask 'How can I do that?' Some of the time could be saved by you only attending a particular part of a meeting rather than sitting through the whole agenda: you ask a colleague (managing across) to brief you on any remaining items which you need to know about. The rest of the time is produced by delegating another meeting to one of your team (i.e. managing downwards).

The 'managing yourself' junction box can also enable you to make the breakthrough about the distinction between urgent and important. Suppose you realise that you are spending too much time away from your team, firefighting problems (urgent). Your team is suffering because you haven't found time to work out a strategy with them (important) — which is one of the reasons why so much firefighting is called for. You need to shift some priority from managing outwards to downwards. For one month, you give a colleague (managing across) the authority to handle the 'outwards' urgent issues without referring back to you. During that month you work with your team to create the clear strategy.

> Redistributing your time through 5-way management is not rocket science. But managers who consciously use the 5-way approach report that it strengthens their determination to make time management work: "it puts you in the driving seat" as one manager commented.

Here are some other simple examples:

- An editor regularly discusses priorities with her immediate boss (managing upwards) and concentrates on these areas, as they are where she can deliver added value. Any new work which occurs which does not rate as a priority is delegated (managing downwards).
- A market promotions manager who has to work on several internal projects with other departments (managing across) was coached in 5-way management and commented, "I realise I need to spend more time planning (managing yourself) rather than rushing in. This should help to achieve what I want, with less compromise."
- Several managers in a housing association were reluctant to delegate anything beyond trivial issues, because they feared that delegation would create a vacuum — colleagues would question how these managers could justify their existence. Understanding 5-way management enabled the managers to see their contribution in perspective. By genuine delegation (managing downwards) they created spaces in which to draw up service level agreements (managing across) to give internal customers an improved service.

Stress

Many recent surveys* have concurred that stress levels at work are alarmingly high, leading to absenteeism, insularity and lack of creativity. As managers, we have a dual responsibility in this context to keep our own stress at a reasonable level and to avoid inflicting stress on others. 5-way management provides a good framework to analyse where our stress is coming from (from our immediate

*Are Managers under stress? (Institute of Management, 1996); The Mind Survey — Stress at work (Mind, 1992); Managing Stress (Managing Best Practice no. 18, The Industrial Society 1995).

manager; from our direct reports; from colleagues; from external organisations?) and to whom we may be unwittingly directing stress.

A certain amount of stress is positively helpful, and some people operate at their very best when deadlines are looming. A rush of adrenaline for a short period can be a pleasurable experience. But prolonged stress is harmful and we are being selfish if we overlook the impact of our own stress on others, manifested in irritability, abruptness and so on.

There are five actions we can take to keep our own stress within civilised bounds:

- **OPERATE AT YOUR OWN ADDED VALUE LEVEL** If you allow yourself to be diverted on to trivial issues, and to procrastinate ("I'll put off writing that big report for another week") you are only fooling yourself and storing up trouble. Great job satisfaction comes from looking back over a week's work and knowing that for much of the time you were delivering what you were uniquely placed to deliver to the organisation and to your team.

- **USE 'MANAGING OUTWARDS' WHEN YOU GET DEPRESSED** We all have times when nothing seems to go right, and it is easy to become sucked into a vicious spiral. You can even start to feel a little paranoid, as if everything is conspiring against you. When this happens, try very hard to make some space in your diary to get away from your normal workplace for a day — go and visit another branch, or a customer or supplier, or accompany a colleague on his travels. This should help to give you a sense of perspective.

- **ASK FOR HELP** The natural ups and downs of working life create problems for everyone sooner or later. It is simply common-sense to recognise this, and should not be regarded as weakness for you to ask for help from colleagues. This help can take all sorts of forms: borrowing a member of another team to overcome a peak of work; negotiating a little extra time on a deadline, and so on. This should not be confused with wimpish failure to pull out extra effort. Who is more childish — the manager who says to colleagues "I'm in difficulty — I need some help" or the one who dares not lose face and produces a shoddy piece of work, accompanied by liberal splashings of blame in all directions?

> "Asking for help or support — and accepting it — is a strategy that confronts the fact that we are not perfect. Some find it more challenging to accept their limitations and ask for help than to struggle on."
>
> **Eve Warren**
> *Empower Yourself*

- **LET OFF STEAM** How you choose to do this is very much a matter of individual preference. Physical exercise suits some people; using a mentor or counsellor helps others; and I know of one manager who installed a punchbag in his office on which he could vent his frustrations without doing any harm to anything other than his wrist (a new version of repetitive strain injury?!)
  Another manager said "Energetic gardening seems to release some of the pressure, and I can recommend pet ownership as very soothing and distracting."
- **FIND OUT THE 'WHY' BEHIND THE 'WHAT'** If I ask you to do something, I stand a much better chance of gaining your wholehearted commitment to it if I give you the reason behind the request. "I need this by Tuesday because ..."; "We have to redraft this in order to ..." So if your manager, or a colleague, or an inspector, makes a request which seems opaque or unreasonable, ask for the background. If you know why, you and your team will be better placed to fulfil the request in the way which will be most helpful to the person making it.

2 managing upwards

This dimension applies to anyone below the very top level in an organisation. Even with the current moves towards flatter structures and self-managed teams, almost everyone still reports to a manager. You may have no choice as to who that manager is, but your relationship will make all the difference to your effectiveness and job satisfaction.

Understanding your manager's job

The first step is to understand the reality of his or her job. On paper, management jobs can be described in straightforward terms and it is revealing to read your manager's job description. (It is surprising how many people have never done this, either because they never thought of doing so or because they are not allowed to!)

But what is even more useful is to gauge the reality of the job — the 'political' overtones, the pressures, the satisfactions; what takes up most time, what interruptions occur, and so on. Your motive for understanding this reality is not nosiness — although there is naturally an element of curiosity — but because the better you appreciate this reality, the greater the chance of working out an effective partnership with your manager. Nowadays the extent of overlap between management levels is tiny compared to a few years ago. This is healthy, but carries the potential danger that each post becomes discrete and isolated. The ideal is that my job, at level 'B', should be clearly defined, with any overlap with my manager's job at level 'A' being deliberate. We both know exactly what we are trying to achieve, some of which will be carried out individually and some jointly. By looking at the reality of the manager's job you can together work out an appropriate synergy.

In this way you can play to each other's strengths. Every manager has some favourite aspects of his work and some corresponding horrors. If you and your manager have an intelligent relationship, you can agree between you who does what, bending the boundaries of your official job descriptions. In this way the organisation's work gets done, and what is more it will be done to a higher standard.

This is not a cavalier abandonment of managerial responsibilities. There are many duties which I should not be allowed to off-load on to someone else even if I will never be brilliant at them. But it is a sensible use of 'horses for courses' and it brings you and your manager into a meaningful partnership.

In a similar way, if you have a thrusting, let's-get-on-with-it approach to management, when you are writing a report for your more cautious manager you will have consciously to adapt your style, to avoid him feeling stampeded. Neither logic alone nor emotion alone persuades people: both are needed. For advice on how to manage various personalities, see Appendix 1.

Occasionally during your career you may be able to manoeuvre yourself into a position where you report to a particularly good manager. But for the most part, it is a matter of luck whether we find our manager a pleasure or a pain to work for.

Even working for bad managers — for a short period — can have it advantages. If you observe them closely you can analyse what they fail to do, or do in the wrong way. This throws up into sharper relief what effective managers do, as a contrast.

If you are unfortunate enough to work for a really noxious manager, you will find that a mentor can provide an invaluable safety valve for your frustrations; and a mentor can also help you to work out ways of coping with your boss to make life more tolerable. (Mentors are not limited to this 'defensive' role, but can be especially worthwhile carrying it out.)

Suppose you report to a reasonably effective manager. What does 'managing upwards' mean in this situation?

First, it is important to understand the demands of her role. The organisation may look quite different when seen from the level above your own. What sort of pressures is your manager under? What deadlines does she have to meet? What political games are being played?

Your understanding of your manager will be greatly helped if you separate out her role from her personal contribution. The tough but realistic approach to role definition is the one which requires every post to be justified from scratch (like the principle of zero-based budgeting). Each post should add something which cannot be provided at the level below. In a supermarket you might start with shelf-fillers and checkout operators (although even these posts are becoming automated.) Could the supermarket run with just these staff and no others? No, other staff are needed to decide which products to sell and what price, etc. In this way every post in the organisation is rigorously validated.

So the first aspect of your manager's contribution is the demands of the post itself. In traditional terms, this is the job description; in less traditional terms, the key result areas or the performance commitments. Is your manager's post similar to your own but with more far-reaching decisions? Or is it altogether different? By such analysis you are able to identify the requirements of your manager's role, regardless of the person occupying it. It is worth considering this carefully; you can be more objective at this stage than at the next.

Your manager's added value skills

Having thought about your manager's role, you can now consider the second part of his contribution to the organisation. What special, individual, even unique skills, experience and abilities does your manager bring to the post? How does he choose to carry it out? What is his management style? Which aspects of the job does he enjoy most? What does he choose to spend most time on? Which aspects are easier for him to carry out than might be expected?

By asking yourself these questions you will distil the personal 'added value' which your manager contributes. If he were run over by a bus tomorrow, it is in the 'added value' area where the difference would be most noticeable: his successor's profile in this area might be totally different, even if the duties of the post continued unchanged.

You need to understand your manager's contribution as a whole, but the real opportunity for the two of you to get on the same wavelength comes from the 'added value' area. By focusing on this, you will be better able to anticipate your manager's reaction to proposals and recommendations. Your own personality may be completely different, and you are not required to like or admire your manager: but it is in your own interest, and the organisation's, that the two of you should make a real effort to work together.

This is even more important in this era of 'delayering'. With no deputies or intermediate levels, managers who used to have four or five direct reports now have twelve or fifteen. If you are one of the twelve, your manager now has considerably less time available for you *individually* even though you may have just as much direct contact as before through team meetings.

So you need to make the most of what you can obtain. The best system is to arrange regular 1:1 meetings with him. Their frequency will depend on the total amount of face-to-face contact you have; if you sit in the next office to your manager you need fewer 1:1's than if you are based thirty miles away at another site. What actually qualifies as a 1:1? There are eight criteria:

1   A private, face-to-face discussion between job holder
    and immediate manager
2   The discussion reviews the whole job, not just a single
    aspect
3   The meeting is structured, not a casual chat
4   The discussion includes past, present and future: the
    usual timescale is up to three months in each direction
5   The results of the meeting are recorded in writing on
    the 1:1 notes
6   Although most of the discussion is about the job
    holder, the manager will invite the job holder to make
    constructive comments on their effectiveness as a
    partnership
7   The 1:1 discussion produces specific action points with
    deadline dates
8   At the end of the discussion, a date is agreed for the
    next full 1:1 and this is entered on the notes

Sometimes 'managing upwards' involves not only
relating to your own manager but a group of managers at
that level. This can take the form of an executive team, or a
board of directors, or the trustees of a voluntary
organisation, or a committee of councillors in local
government. The company secretary, or equivalent, learns
the skills of dealing harmoniously with groups of this
kind.

Emotions can run high in their meetings, commonly
because:

1   each participant feels they have to defend their own
    corner and
2   they often lack experience of other functions. It is still
    not unknown for a board to include a sales director
    whose whole life has been in sales, a finance director
    who has never left the finance function, and so on.

In addition to the legal aspects, the main point to grasp
is the overriding difference between directors and
managers — responsibility for strategy and the long term

rather than day-to-day management. This difference is dealt with later in chapter six.

Ambition and promotion

A further reason why you may wish to study your manager's job closely is ambition. There is nothing wrong with that, so long as you a not actually planning a *coup d'état*! But it is important to be aware of some key factors.

1   The lack of overlap between management levels means that promotion may place you in a markedly different type of role: one whose demands may not be congenial, and which is quite unlike the traditional move up a notch to a bigger version of your previous post.

2   In aiming for promotion, you may have a clear picture of the post you wish to fill, but that is only half the story. A managerial job embraces both content and context. The duties of the post may suit you perfectly, but what about the colleagues you will find yourself working with? You can no doubt quickly think of a manager whom you know, ideally qualified for his or her job but unhappy because of a poor fit with colleagues; and probably also of another manager, who grapples with a difficult job which is made ten times less fraught because of marvellously supportive colleagues.

3   Sometimes promotion as such will not be in your own long-term interests. A very able young manager in a large food company was offered promotion to a post at group headquarters. He declined, asking instead to be sent to manage a run-down depot in an unattractive area. His friends thought him crazy but he turned the depot into a much more successful unit — then asked for his move to head office, where he ended up in charge of the group's strategic planning. His reasoning was that he needed first-hand experience of life a long way from the artificial luxuries of a group headquarters, and he claimed that this experience

indeed proved invaluable; when preparing strategic plans he could root them in reality.

If you have to make proposals to such groups, whether in writing or in person, the best single piece of advice is to demonstrate awareness of the *all-round* implications of your theme. If you work in a hospital, and are recommending the purchase of a piece of equipment, your proposal will stand a stronger chance of acceptance if you show that you have considered its effects on the X-ray department *and* the operating theatre, etc. In other words, make what might be called the 'business case' rather than the 'departmental case'.

Workshadowing

A very simple method for understanding the reality of posts one level above your own is workshadowing. You arrange to accompany a manager constantly over a short period, usually a couple of days, or perhaps each afternoon for a week. It is important to be present at every activity (except any which are too sensitive, e.g. a disciplinary interview) in order to absorb the full flavour of the manager's work. You can learn as much from the way she deals with unplanned interruptions as well as with formal meetings.

The basis of workshadowing is that you are a silent observer. At intervals the manager discusses with you how she handled the events of the day, supplying the 'why' to illuminate the 'what'. You will learn much about the manager's role and her added value: often the reality of the post is far removed from its image. More often than not, it turns out that the manager has less absolute authority than might have appeared, and has to work through persuasion and influence rather than through issuing orders. Many managers' work is remarkably fragmented and reactive. A few hours of workshadowing can be mutually rewarding: it is uncommon for the senior manager to find the shadow's questions insignificant.

If your present position is one or perhaps two levels below the board of directors (or equivalent), and there is a reasonable prospect of your being promoted to board level, it is vital to become thoroughly familiar with the responsibilities of directors in advance of your promotion. When you become a director you immediately acquire special legal responsibilities, and many directors receive remarkably scant induction to their new posts. Only 16% of internally promoted and only 10% of externally recruited directors receive formal training on their legal duties. As regards the board's strategic role, 27% of directors are expected to 'pick it up as they go along'; and only 20% of boards regularly evaluate their own effectiveness*

The 'label' which we acquire as a functional specialist tends to hang round our neck right through our career. A few years ago Sir Peter Baxendell was promoted to be chief executive of Shell in the UK. There are few larger jobs than that. Yet the *Financial Times* reported, "Sir Peter Baxendell, a petroleum engineer, has been appointed chief executive …". I am quite certain that Sir Peter had long ceased to think of himself as a petroleum engineer — indeed you cannot act, and be seen to act, as an effective general manager or director without sloughing off any special loyalty to a particular function in the business.

---

* *Director Development, Managing Best Practice No. 23, The Industrial Society*

3 managing downwards

People as an infinite resource

The list of resources with which a manager is entrusted includes several similar elements regardless of the organisation. A typical list covers: premises, equipment, materials, money, time, information, goodwill, and people. In what way are the last two different in kind from all of the others? Their potential is infinite, while all of the rest have a limit.

Goodwill is a neglected resource: it includes your organisation's reputation, its style, spirit and character. The way in which an organisation handles a mistake or complaint can deplete or reinforce the goodwill resource literally overnight.

The people resource is even more powerful, and can encompass individuals who are not even on your payroll. For example a good school will be able to mobilise parents and ex-students in all sorts of ways; most hospitals have a league of friends; companies which lend staff to help the local community find that this is repaid many times over.

You only have to look at the voluntary sector to see the power of commitment. Volunteers who help Oxfam or the National Autistic Society do so because they care deeply about what those organisations stand for. Managers outside the voluntary sector can learn from that. If we could show that every one of our employees is working at their full potential from the day they join to the day they leave, our organisation would be truly world class.

So the reason for developing our people need have little

to do with sentiment — it springs from cool logic. A manager is responsible for getting the best out of all his resources; of these the resource with limitless potential is people. Factories used to refer to their employees as 'hands' and the expression 'all hands on deck' perpetuates this. But people have more than hands to contribute: they have a head and a heart as well. Hands can be replaced by robots. For the foreseeable future, heads (brains) will not be overtaken by computers, and the heart (commitment, passion, will, energy) would be hard to imitate. So as managers we have a treble opportunity to:

1   **Recognise the unique potential of our people**
2   **Create the environment where their heads are more important than their hands**
3   **Respect, cherish and align with their hearts**

Several years ago at a school speech day, I heard the guest of honour give a talk which was so compelling that you could have heard a toffee paper drop in the audience. The speaker was Mia Kellmer Pringle, director of the National Children's Bureau, who had spent years studying children. She had gradually become convinced that for their healthy development, all children need:

- **Love**
- **Responsibility**
- **Praise and recognition**
- **Stimulating new experiences**

If these are true of us when we are children, they must remain valid for us as adults. So how can we as managers provide these four features to the members of our teams?

LOVE
Love sounds like a tall order — perhaps even totally inappropriate. But not if we mean love in the sense of getting to know each person as an individual, what makes

him tick, his hopes and fears; and seeing in him potential which he does not see in himself.

RESPONSIBILITY

Responsibility means letting him operate at his added value level: urging him beyond his comfort zone into the stretch zone, but not beyond into the panic zone.

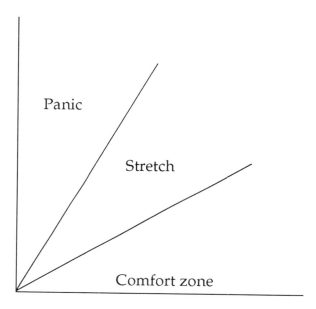

PRAISE AND RECOGNITION

Praise and recognition — Feedback, little and often, is one of the best — and most cost effective! — motivators. When one of your team does something exceptional, as well as thanking her in person, write her a note, put it on her personal file and send a copy to your own manager. (This should also be done when a colleague in another department has pulled out all the stops for you). This is one of the most neglected management habits.

Recognition also means recognising when one of your people is under strain, or unhappy, or not her usual self. You don't have to become an amateur psychologist — just show that you have noticed, and offer any help; without making a big issue of it.

STIMULATING NEW EXPERIENCES

Stimulating new experiences is best approached by considering the individuals and the team as a whole. Sometimes you will be able to freshen up one person, e.g. by a slight change of job content, or by an external visit, or helping her to try one of the fifty ways to personal development.* Sometimes the team as a whole need stimulus: a party, a project, a fund raising challenge for charity. Have we lost our capacity for making work fun?

Matching people and roles

We tend to indulge in wishful thinking when we appoint people to posts. Even if we have gone to the trouble of compiling a detailed job description and a person specification, how often do we find a candidate who exactly matches what we reckon the job requires? So we appoint a person who from the start is to some extent a misfit, and hope that gradually, through experience and training, he or she will become a good fit.

Contrast this with what happens when a really valuable person leaves or retires. Colleagues comment: "He made the job his own. There will never be another Jim". This is because the outgoing job holder has gradually moulded the role to fit like a glove. Typically such people are not only highly respected for their achievements, but noticeably fulfilled in carrying out their role.

Traditionally the process of matching roles and people starts with the role and squeezes the person into it, like a fat man contorting himself into a narrow telephone kiosk. It is uncomfortable, and its shows. This approach derives from the Taylorian work-study mindset. It is as though the work which the organisation needs to get done fits into a huge crate: inside this are many smaller boxes, each of precise dimensions (jobs), and together all the boxes make a perfect fit into the huge crate, with no flexibility.

*See Appendix 5

The more liberating approach is to start with the people, not the jobs. Look at each person as a truly unique human being. Just as no two people have an identical DNA profile, so no two people have the same combination of talents, aspirations, strengths and weaknesses. Every one of us is a funny shape: and in addition we can change our shape, like a jelly.

In the perfect company, all these funny shapes would add up to the overall shape of the company, i.e. everything the company needed to have done would be done, and what is more it would be achieved by totally fulfilled people, each one in a tailor-made, ideal job.

This is not as far fetched as it may look at first sight. Clearly you cannot move from the "jobs as boxes" approach to the "people as jellies" approach overnight. But you can go a considerable distance towards it.

In Kirklees Metropolitan Borough Council, heads of service are regularly appraised throughout the year. Among the topics on which they are targeted are their added value as individuals, both personal and service performance indicators and their personal contribution to the corporate body.*

Delegation — The R/A/D system

Every manager seems to be in favour of delegation in principle, but many find it difficult to put into practice. A simple and effective method is the one which was originally created by BICC, the electronics and construction company. It works like this:

> You ask one of your direct reports to write down all the decisions which *regularly* crop up in his job. (This does not include 'one-off' special situations). It is convenient if these are clustered under themes, e.g.

*Employee empowerment in local government — panacea or poppycock? The Belgrave Papers no.11, Local Government Management Board.

the 'Staffing' list might include items such as 'Recruit
staff up to grade 4 within budgeted numbers'
'Authorise overtime working' etc.

Alongside the list he should draw three columns headed
'Recommend', 'Act', and 'Delegate'.

The two of you then go through the whole list and agree
for each item a tick to go in one of the three columns,
which are self-explanatory: 'Recommend' means that when
this decision arises, your direct report comes to you with a
recommended course of action but may not go further
without your agreement. 'Act' simply means that he makes
the decision himself; 'Delegate' means that he is
transferring the decision to someone below his level, so the
decision need no longer appear on his own list.

The R/A/D System

JOB TASK	RECOMMEND	ACT	DELEGATE
Budgeting figures	√		
Training schedule			√
Stationery supplies		√	

For all these decisions the intention is steadily to push
them towards the right: R→A→D. When newly appointed,
your direct report can expect to have many ticks in the
'Recommend' column. As he gains experience these should
be shifting across to 'Act' and subsequently to 'Delegate'.

This R/A/D system becomes still more interesting and
fruitful if you have several direct reports doing similar
work. They compile the list together and go through it
with you as a group. A given decision may then be
allocated to the 'R' column for James, who is new to the
job; to 'A' for Sarah and Leslie, who are more experienced,
and to 'D' for Barbara who has handled it many times.

A further variation of this system, which clears your own
desk even more effectively, is for James to take any items in
his 'Recommend' column not to you but to his colleague
Barbara, who coaches him in moving from R to A. As

manager of the team, you can scan the columns to see where the ticks fall for each person. If James has still kept most of the ticks under 'R' some months after starting the job, perhaps he needs some help to build his confidence; if Leslie has masses of items under 'A' it is time he learned to delegate more of them; and so on.

What, how and why

Managers whom people positively enjoy working for — and no, they are not yet extinct — are those who use a deceptively simple mantra: What, how and why. They achieve a sensible balance between these three.

They start by recognising that people can only become committed if they understand both what and why. If I shout at you "Go outside into the car park immediately!" you will respond with greater alacrity if I add "… because the paint store is on fire." — I have supplied the 'why' as well as the 'what'.

This need can become particularly evident when plans are being prepared. A small group of managers go into a huddle for several hours and emerge to announce 'The Plan.' It either contains masses of *What* but precious little *How*, so that people regard it as unrealistic (and then find all sorts of ingenious ways of scuppering it); or masses of *What* and too much *How*, so that the recipients feel that they have been presented with a *fait accompli*. In both versions the important omission is the *Why*. This is nothing short of tragic, because the managers who went into the huddle are not impulsive fools; they argued hard about Why and considered several alternatives.

The problem is that once you have emerged from the tough undergrowth of *Why*, you are so relieved to have reached the clearing and decided *What* to do that the *Why* becomes a phase you have put behind you. However the staff who will be affected by your plan have not been with you on your journey. To be committed to your plan they need to know *Why*.

Let us look at two practical applications of the balance between *What, How* and *Why*:

1 **Job descriptions**
2 **The minutes of meetings.**

Job Descriptions

Many job descriptions are still turgid to read. If a job description were a cook's recipe, its ingredients might typically be:

> three parts *What*
> six parts *How*
> one part *Why*

The *What* identifies the main responsibilities, the *How* goes into great detail about methods to be used to achieve them, and there is minimal explanation of *Why* the job exists in the first place. The net result is a great deal about inputs, not enough about outcomes: an over-prescriptive document leaving the job holder little scope to show initiative.

The same job could be described much more dynamically if it contained

> four parts *What*
> four parts *Why*
> two parts *How*

This description would give more background on why the job matters and the impact it should make. The tone would be stimulating and challenging. The job holder would understand his contribution and feel he had space to tackle the work his way, so long as he achieved the outcomes.

Minutes of meetings

The second example concerns minutes of meetings. Very often many people who have not personally attended a meeting will nevertheless be affected by its decisions. Sometimes this will happen through their receiving a set of the minutes; in other cases they may not see the minutes as such but will be on the receiving end of some communication resulting from the meeting's decisions.

Time and again the minutes of meetings are expressed as

> six parts *What*
> three parts *How*
> one part *Why*

To a person not present at the *discussion*, the *decision* is all that comes across — and naturally the person's first question is 'Why?' Why should we change the system? Why have they decided on X rather than Y? Why don't they consider us at our branch? Why is head office always given priority? Why are they spending £20,000 on that project but only £4,000 on mine? and so on.

What, How and Why are particularly relevant in achieving change. Think of the change as a journey: we start with *Why*...

Why do we need to embark on this journey in the first place? Can't we stay where we are? —
No because...
Now I see (reluctantly) the need for a change, the sense in making the journey. What is our destination? Where do you want us to end up? —

We need to have reached this point by this date, and to have X and Y up and running. —
So tell me how you want me to get there. —

As long as you are clear on the destination, I'm sure you have your own ideas on the route or routes we could follow. Please think about them and let's talk again.

This sort of dialogue still involves the manager making much of the running. She has carried out the initial analysis

(the *Why*) and has decided on the destination (the *What*).
She has delegated the choice of route (the *How*) to her team.

An Empowered organisation

This approach can be a sensible stepping-stone towards
much stronger involvement by the team, namely through
empowerment. In delegation, the *How* becomes the team's
responsibility. In empowerment, the *What* and the *How* are
taken on by the team. They are enabled to do this through
a fuller understanding of the *Why*. Companies which have
made progress on empowerment report that training in
problem-solving and other analytical skills forms a key
part of the approach. Rather than wait for specialists to
present them with facts and figures, employees are able to
carry out their own analysis (*Why* are customer complaints
increasing? *Why* did it take longer than expected to launch
that new service?) and thus to determine *What* needs to be
done about it, and *How*.

In an empowered organisation, teams can pace their
own increase in responsibilities. In a survey on self-
managed teams*, SC Johnson Wax describe how each of
their teams has a 'custodian' "who agrees the boundaries
of the team's responsibilities with the employees and
specialists across the organisation ... as the teams become
more skilled in working on their chosen categories, so the
boundaries are moved out and the teams' and individuals'
authority and responsibility are increased. With teams at
different stages of development at any one time, each will
decide how far it wants to take the process".

As a method of understanding the reality of a post,
workshadowing has been outlined in the chapter on
managing upwards. But it is not limited to that direction.
You might usefully sit alongside one of your team for a
morning, listening to her deal with queries on the
telephone in order to experience the reality of her work.

---

* *Self Managed Teams, Managing Best Practice No. 11, The Industrial Society
1995*

But a bolder example, going beyond workshadowing to carrying out the entire job comes from the Employment Service, where for a whole week a large Jobcentre in London was run by 70 senior managers from the regional office. This experiment, and its outcomes is described in Appendix 2.

Skills audit

Perhaps — a sign of the times — one of your team joined your organisation after redundancy elsewhere. In her previous company she developed considerable skills at X, but her present work is about Y. It is all too easy for us to forget people's previous experience, or to fail to connect their 'home' skills with their 'work' agenda. Women who return to work after bringing up a family are often too modest about their achievements in planning, budgeting, negotiating, conciliating, arbitration, assertiveness and sheer stamina.

Managers who are really effective in this context make a point of carrying out an annual skills audit. The object is to ensure that you and your team are all up-to-date on the talents possessed within the team. The audit will include a check on

- any new qualifications acquired
- new experience, e.g. through secondments, workshadowing, projects
- awards and prizes won
- significant achievements outside work, e.g. becoming secretary of a voluntary organisation, or captain of the tennis club, or producer of the play in the village hall
- taking office e.g. as a councillor, magistrate, etc. (a few years ago in Leeds, a school dinner lady became Lord Mayor (sic) in her own right)
- any 'firsts' achieved by individuals, such as the first time this person hosted a group of visitors, or made a speech, or led a working party, etc.

There are many options for how to carry out the skills audit. People can update their career history held in Personnel Records, or go through a checklist individually with you in their 1:1 meetings, or prompt each other in pairs and then list everything on flipcharts in a team meeting. Once you have gathered the new information you may wish to use it as the basis for a celebration of some sort — a teambuilding occasion, congratulating the team on its progress towards lifelong learning.

Coaching

All of us as managers seem to take it for granted that we are natural coaches. But coaching is a subtle skill which we owe it to our teams to perfect. In his excellent book *Coaching for Performance*, John Whitmore makes it clear that a coach aims to increase a person's awareness of his performance and his responsibility for it. Screaming at a learner "try harder!" is not coaching.

The coach has to see the task not through his own eyes but through the learner's. Thus it is a great help to find out whether the two of you have the same natural styles of looking at issues, and tackling problems.

Various diagnostic instruments are available to help you to do this. Amongst these are:

- The Strength Deployment Inventory [SDI]. The Strength Deployment Inventory assesses personal strengths under two conditions: when things are going well and when faced with conflict and opposition. It provides insight into styles of relating to others and sources of personal gratification in relationships. Plotting the scores of individual team members on a triangular grid enables you to highlight comparisons.
- The learning styles questionnaire developed by Peter Honey and Alan Mumford. By answering eighty

questions [there are no 'right' or 'wrong' answers] your preferred style of learning can be summarised under headings:

- **Activist**
- **Pragmatist**
- **Reflector**
- **Theorist**

What becomes really useful is for an individual and her manager to become aware of each other's learning styles — if 'A', a theorist, is trying to coach 'B', an activist, 'B' is likely to get impatient, preferring to learn by trial and error.

Decision making

You may find it difficult, as do many managers, to work out when to make decisions yourself and when to consult your team about them. Here we can learn from two highly effective leaders in different fields. The first is General Colin Powell, American military Chief of Staff, who has had to make a greater number of (literally) life and death decisions than you or I have had hot dinners. In his autobiography he describes his approach as follows:

"I developed a decision making philosophy. Put simply, it is to dig up all the information you can, then go with your instincts. ... I use my intellect to inform my instinct. Then I use my instinct to test all this data. However, we do not have the luxury of collecting information indefinitely. At some point, before we can have every possible fact in hand, we have to decide. The key is not to make quick decisions, but to make timely decisions. I have a timing formula, P=40 to 70, in which P stands for probability of success and the numbers indicate the percentage of information acquired. I don't act if I only have enough information to give me less than a 40% chance of being right.

> **And I don't wait until I have enough facts to be 100% sure of being right, because by then it is almost always too late. I go with my gut feeling when I have acquired information somewhere in the range of 40%–70%."**
>
> **Colin Powell**
> *A Soldier's Way*

The second is the chief executive of a large group of companies in the financial services sector. I helped him run a workshop for his top management team. He had been appointed from outside, and although he had met all of his top team individually the workshop was the first occasion on which they had all come together with him. His opening statement to them included this:

"My first impressions of the company are very favourable in some ways, but it's clear we will also have to make some important changes in the coming months. As chief executive I will take full responsibility for these changes. But I want your input — I am not infallible.

"Our approach will be like this: I will propose a change which I am provisionally going to make. I will specify an 'open season' — a period of (say) a month, during which I want comments from all of you about my idea. You can say it's the worst idea you've ever heard of — so long as you have an alternative to suggest. I will listen hard to all of your comments.

"At the end of the 'open season', if I want to go ahead with the change, we will have a 'close season' for a specified length of time. During this period I want you to try your hardest to make the new system work. I want your wholehearted commitment to it — no muttering, no sabotage, go for it. At the end of this trial period we will have a second, brief, 'open season' during which we will review the change. Is it working? Can we improve on it?

Should we forget the whole thing? During this open season you can tell me 'I told you it wouldn't work' or 'It would work better like this' and so on.

"At the end of this open season I will make a final decision one way or the other — and as you will have had not one but two opportunities to give me your views, this time it will be a final version with no ifs or buts, and with your full blooded enthusiasm."

This strikes me as very civilised. Here is a top manager genuinely consulting people but not shirking his personal ultimate responsibility.

A different example comes from a police force: when top management have reached a decision to introduce a new policy, this is outlined to police officers at all levels face-to-face by their sub-division officer. They are invited to 'fine tune' the new policy and comment on it, although the principle behind it cannot be altered. Their views are then relayed to the top levels.

4 managing across the organisation

The least productive period of my career was spent at the head office of a group of companies. If you could have measured the creative energy produced in that building, it would have gone off the scale. Unfortunately ninety per cent was internecine: backstabbing was rife, and departments seemed more interested in damaging each other than damaging the company's competitors.

That company no longer exists, but you may know of others where collaboration is conspicuous by its absence. The transformation, as always, needs to come from the top, but the reasons for such a poor atmosphere often turn out to be simple (not simple = easy to put right but simple = straightforward). They may be a combination of corporate and individual issues.

Individual Relationships

At the corporate level, clarity of structure is achieved by splitting an organisation into functional departments. This looks good on an organisation chart but its designers need to remember that synergy between departments can only result from *individual* relationships.

At the individual level, the problem can be that two people see the world in different ways: sometimes our professional training encourages this, e.g. auditors and IT specialists look for mismatches (discrepancies, software bugs) whereas designers and personnel managers seek the opposite (fitness for purpose, whether in a product or a person).

Or we may have had one unhelpful encounter with a specialist from another discipline and generalise this into a maxim ("All marketing people are arrogant, and some are even more so" was the slogan on the wall in one production manager's office). Or we may simply not understand another speciality but are afraid of showing our ignorance, so we rationalise this into a need to keep our distance ("No point in discussing this with X department, they are on another planet").

The only beneficiaries from these behaviours are our competitors. We have to go back to basics to establish a new way for departments to work together, and this is often the point at which an independent facilitator can provide the crucial assistance.

Psychometric instruments such as the Myers-Briggs Type Indicator (MBTI)* can come into play. Whatever specific techniques are used, the new relationship is achieved through these three stages.:

- Commitment to a goal which is "bigger than both of us". This has to be something only attainable by co-operation — really challenging but not impossible. It must be seen to be worthwhile, and defined precisely, with milestones.
- Understanding each other's approach. This includes a general appreciation of the person's speciality, i.e. their professional stance; and how they as an individual approach issues, i.e. their personal frame of reference. People usually need help to articulate this, because by

*Myers-Briggs Type Indicator (MBTI). Through a thirty minute questionnaire you can assess your preferred style of working with and interacting with other people. Your preference is measured on four dimensions:

- Extraversion — introversion
- Sensing — intuition
- Thinking — feeling
- Judging — perception

definition our personal approach simply feels right and natural. Sometimes people are genuinely surprised to find that there are different ways of looking at issues.

- Agreeing 'ground rules' for working together. The most important of these will include requests and promises. "A" makes a request that X is done by a given date. "B" responds either by accepting, declining or making an alternative offer. The aim here is to avoid the charade of making a promise which you have no realistic hope of achieving, and which leads to endless ingenuity in spreading the blame.

Putting relationships on to a new footing requires determination and resilience, but we are fooling ourselves if we keep finding reasons why it cannot be done.

Flatter structures

In recent years much attention, arguably overdue, has been given to streamlining management structures vertically, i.e. reducing to the minimum the number of levels between the chief executive and front-line staff. Commonly several layers of management have been removed and communication both upwards and downwards has been considerably speeded up. At the same time there has been increased emphasis on cross-functional working, e.g. in project teams whose life is limited to the timespan of the project itself.

One implication of flatter structures is that traditional promotion systems are obsolete. Narrow promotional routes through one function — often called silos or chimneys — are now inadequate. Each manager has to oversee a wider variety of specialisms. (In a few organisations, career structures now enable specialists to move up their own career ladder without having to become managers at all.)

So on sheer mathematical grounds, your opportunities

for vertical promotion have been reduced. This makes it all the more vital that you understand the demands of your manager's role (see chapter 2) if you are to aspire to filling it. It may therefore be in your interest to spend some time — perhaps through a secondment or on a project team — working closely with your colleagues who report to the same manager as yourself. It is not only in your own interests but those of the organisation that as a candidate for promotion you should have experienced (say) three types of work within your broad function rather than only one.

The second implication applies irrespective of whether or not you are interested in promotion. The organisation's ability to achieve synergy, to make 2+2=5, depends on people working harmoniously across the organisation. 'Harmoniously' does not mean a bogus cosiness in which disagreements are unknown and ideas are never challenged. But it does mean the left hand knowing what the right hand is doing, and especially it means people being aware of how, by collaborating, they can improve service to their customers, whether internal or external. I find it astounding how in many organisations, departments operate as if in sealed capsules, either blissfully ignorant of or simply not interested in what their colleagues are doing — until they crash into each other.

In some organisations formal steps have been taken to overcome this. In local government and the national health service there is extensive use of service level agreements. These can be designed either for internal or external relationships. Post Office Counters Ltd describe Service Level Agreements (SLAs) as follows:

Service Level Agreement — A Simple Definition

A Service Level Agreement (SLA) formalises the standards, scope and purpose of the service which has been established and agreed between the supplier and the customer and acts as an on-going

---

measure of service provision and customer satisfaction. Within the framework of the agreement, the following key elements may be included:-

The services to be provided: specific customer requirements; the supplier and customer responsibilities; costs for the provision of the service; key measurables; issues on management of change; review mechanisms; forecast timescales and authorised customer and supplier signatories.

Although it is perfectly possible to tackle the two things separately, the preferred approach is to make measuring customer satisfaction an integral part of the SLA process ... particularly if the SLA addresses a service of critical importance to the customer, where continuous improvement is possible and highly desirable. This means not only measuring performance against each of the requirements specified in the SLA, but also measuring the customer's satisfaction with each area of performance.

Agreements can take a number of forms, for example:

(a) In a Project environment the formal "contract" which is already produced between the project sponsor and project manager includes in great detail the elements required for a SLA. There may, in a project environment, be more than one SLA; for example between the project manager and 'supplier teams' providing technical/planning/ systems resource to the project; between the project manager and sponsor; or between project manager and the recipients of the project deliverables.

(b) In areas where pieces of consultancy are generally fairly short-lived or one-off activities.

(c) Between a section and its sponsor. Such an SLA would clarify roles and responsibilities; work areas sponsored; monitoring and feedback arrangements and so on.

(d) In 'processes' as an integral part of a process performance management system linked to critical areas within the overall process.

A flexible approach, which meets both customers' and suppliers' requirements and adopts that which is most suitable in the circumstances should be the key.

Why are SLAs important? ... A SLA encapsulates, in a simple document, the fundamentals of effective working relationships between customers and suppliers. Without such an agreement there is lack of purpose, unclear customer requirements, and scope for considerable ambuguity. The SLA approach does not add complexity — it focuses customer and supplier on agreeing what is important and how it is to be delivered and measured.

What are the benefits for customer and supplier? ... There are several important benefits for both parties, including ... a clear, prioritised understanding of customer requirements; a change mechanism that minimises the likelihood of unagreed changes to customer requirements; and the establishment of formal communication channels between customer and supplier.

Who needs to know about and use SLAs? ... All supplier teams providing important internal services need to understand and employ the SLA approach. Customer teams receiving services critical to their objectives should fully understand the approach and the benefits it can bring. Business Unit Leaders and other senior managers need a general understanding of the SLA process.

Another effective device is the objectives/support grid.

This is very simple, but produces practical results. The way to use it is as follows:

You sit round the table with three colleagues from other departments. On the table is an A3 sized grid. You write your name at 'A' and your colleagues' names at 'B', 'C' and 'D'. First you describe the main objectives which your own department is working towards. The headings of these objectives are entered on the grid at A/A (headings only — not the full detail.) Your colleagues follow suit and their objectives are summarised at B/B, C/C and D/D.

You then ask each colleague in turn what support his department can provide to help you achieve your objectives. This is summarised in the appropriate squares on the grid — support to A by B, C and D. During your dialogue with B, the other two colleagues C and D listen and join in as necessary: for example if B is playing 'hard to get' or has run out of ideas; or if they feel he is being unrealistic in the offers he makes to you.

The most fruitful support to capture goes beyond routines which are already happening (e.g. my department sends you a report of stock levels every Tuesday afternoon) and concentrates on what will make a difference:

- what is not happening at all
- what could be speeded up
- what could be produced more frequently
- what would provide early warning of problems
- what figures would be more useful 'approximate, but quick' rather than 'accurate, but slow'
- which person in department B has never actually met the person in department A with whom they have considerable contact by memo or telephone
- which piece of information takes time to produce and has outlived its real value
- what decisions is B making, without checking on their implications on A
- what new work has A moved on to, of which B was unaware
- what duplication of effort is going on
- what wheels are being reinvented
- what training do B's staff need to provide A with a better service
- what joint activities should be undertaken
- which conflicting priorities need to be 'refereed' by the manager one level up from A and B
- what personal relationships could be improved between A's team and B's
- what improvements in customer service could result if only A and B were to get their act together
- what activity, currently working well between A and B, should now be extended to C

It is best not to clutter the grid with too much detail. It may not be worth recording every way in which one department supports another, but rather to focus on:

- **new ways in which support is required**
- **opportunities to improve relationships**
- **areas requiring a special thrust e.g., for a limited period of time**
- **areas where routine support has lapsed and new standards need to be established**
- **areas which could have a marked impact on customer service**

This discussion produces commitments of *mutual* support between A, B, C and D: thus all sixteen squares on the grid have something specific written in.

This is how a Resources Manager in a voluntary organisation described the process:

"I undertook a series of liaison meetings with other departments in order to discuss the information services provided by my department and ask:

1   whether they still require the service/information.
2   whether they require it in the format/style provided.
3   whether it would be helpful if the service/information was provided in a different style/format and at a different time.
4   whether there were other services/information that would be helpful to them in achieving their objectives. As my objective is to help them achieve theirs, these meetings identified areas of mutual support and effected closer more helpful future liaison which helped my team become more efficient.

During my liaison meetings with colleagues I identified two colleagues who were thinking along the same lines as myself in developing an IT system for Resources Information. We developed this as an offshoot of the liaison meetings and successfully replaced a paper based system with an IT one which resulted in efficiency savings for the organisation."

Occasionally, no matter how hard you try, two departments simply cannot identify any worthwhile support between each other.

If so they can cross out the relevant square. Similarly in a few cases it would not be proper for two departments to work closely – e.g. in the financial services sector or in legal firms, where two partners may be representing rival clients in a take-over bid. In these cases 'Chinese walls' take precedence and the grid is of no help.

During the discussions between A,B,C and D, it is common for other actions to emerge which need to be taken by E, F etc., who are not present at the meeting. These should be noted and taken up with those concerned afterwards.

The follow up to the discussion takes this shape. First, a full version of the support which has been committed should be written up (the A3 grid only has space for headings); this can be put in a ring binder of which A,B,C and D each have a copy. Second, you obviously need to brief members of your department on the outcomes of the meeting, and B,C and D do likewise with their teams. Third, the four colleagues agree to meet again at reasonable intervals and review progress. If the system is proving its worth, you may want to extend the grid to include E and F — it then becomes $6 \times 6 = 36$ squares; a seventh department brings the total to 49, and so on.

There comes a stage when to extend the grid any further (twelve departments = 144 squares!) seems absurd. But although you might not want to complete the grid in a monster meeting on this scale, it may nevertheless be worth producing the outcomes in another way — for instance by running a smaller grid discussion as a demonstration, with other managers listening and observing. They then go off in fours and produce their own grids, which are used as the basis for the jumbo-sized version. The remaining gaps are filled using common sense to determine how many people need to have discussions together.

Whatever the size of the objectives/support grid, it should yield a number of important results:

- It should eliminate unnecessary information — you no longer need to send memos to people who are not involved
- It should eliminate misunderstandings and reduce unnecessary friction between departments
- It should improve planning, by one department being more aware of the knock-on effects on another
- For the manager one level up from managers A,B,C and D the grid is invaluable in showing the inter-

departmental contacts which are taking place. This
manager can use the grid when carrying out 1:1
discussions with managers A,B,C and D, and at the
time of the annual appraisal. It is a particularly useful
tool if 360° appraisal is used (see chapter eight).

Benefits from using the objectives/ support grid

1   **Clarity**
    Each manager knows clearly the objectives of her
    colleagues.
2   **Collaboration**
    Each manager is committed to providing specific
    support, and in return can expect specific support.
3   **Meetings**
    Meetings can be constructed for small groups of people
    who are involved with a particular objective, instead of
    larger numbers who are not needed.
4   **Workload**
    The manager one level up from these department
    heads (M1) can use the grid to check on underload or
    overload of work. He can urge the "I've only got time
    for my own problems" manager into greater co-
    operation, and the "I've all the time in the world to
    help others" manager into keeping his eye on the ball.
5   **Budgets**
    The grid contributes to better budgeting. The M1 can,
    if desire, split up objectives amongst her team by
    requiring each manager to contribute something
    measurable in the form of support to a colleague. For
    example, manager "A" is the co-ordinator of a
    particular objective, and his department is accountable
    for producing 80% of the total required to fulfil it. But
    the remaining 20% could be produced by other
    departments — say 15% from "B" and 5% from "C".

6 **Customer care**

One of the most frequent complaints from customers is that the left hand in an organisation doesn't appear to know what the right hand is doing. The grid helps to overcome this by revealing incompatible objectives and by emphasising the support required by one department from another.

5 managing outwards

External Contacts

The range of your contacts, actual and potential, outside your organisation is vast. You need to have a strategy for each type of contact, otherwise you are forced on to the defensive, always reacting to others' initiatives.

Many managers with whom I discuss this issue have never actually listed their external contacts and are somewhat taken aback when they realise their extent. If you work for a company your list could look like this:

- Customers
- Suppliers
- Regulators and auditors
- Inspectors and assessors
- Bankers
- Solicitors
- Surveyors, architects and other professional advisers
- Research establishments
- Benchmarking visits
- Media
- Government — Local
- Government — Central
- The community
- Competitors
- Potential employees
- Schools, colleges and universities
- Trade association, chamber of commerce etc.
- Professional institutes

- Retired employees
- Consultants

Obviously the specifics of your strategy for dealing with each of these external contacts will depend on the nature of your work. But a general point from which to start is that by their very nature, some of these contacts are much easier to influence than others.

There are three categories:

1   Contacts where you have total or near total freedom. This will include whom you select as your *suppliers*; whom you recruit as new *employees*; which *schools, colleges or universities* you collaborate with, e.g. to provide recruits or to carry out sponsored research; which *professional advisers* (bankers, solicitors, surveyors, etc.) you use.

2   Contacts where you have some choice, but not so much. This will include *trade associations, Chambers of Commerce*, etc. (because only some will be relevant by the nature of your business or for geographical reasons); the local *community* in places where you operate (you have some choice in how actively you participate in local affairs); and the *media* — you cannot stop them featuring you in news items, but you can choose how pro-active to be towards them. Also in this category are *local and national government*: you cannot opt out of the laws of the land, but you have a choice about active lobbying etc.

3   Contacts which you are saddled with, whether you like it or not: *regulators and auditors*, inspectors and assessors. These range from the regulators for your business sector (Personal Investment Authority, Ofsted, etc.), to your financial auditors, health and safety inspectors, environmental inspectors, VAT inspectors, Customs and Excise — no doubt you sometimes wonder how you get any 'real work' done at all!

But in fact even the compulsory inspections can be turned to good account. If your organisation passes an inspection with flying colours, this does not happen by a fluke. It will have been the result of sustained hard work and attention to detail, not just by a few specialists but by staff across wide swathes of the organisation. So why not make something of it? Communicate the outcomes of the inspection; give credit where it is due to the people involved; highlight the areas needing improvement, and produce an action plan to make next year's inspection even more favourable.

> **5-way management provides the structure to enable this to happen. A report by an external inspector or assessor (i.e. managing outwards) leads to communication of the results (downwards and across) and to an action plan involving several departments (across) which will be of considerable interest to top management (upwards).**

Although your 'managing outwards' strategy will depend on your type of business, some points will apply generally. These include the following:

CUSTOMERS

> **Our old friend the 80/20 rule can be very helpful. When you analyse your customer base you find that 80% of your profits come from 20% of your customers. It simply may not be profitable, in fact quite the reverse, to add new customers if they buy trivial amounts of your product or service. You only have to look at advertising agencies to see how vulnerable they can be if they lose a major client when the contract comes up for renewal and they have to take part in a 'beauty contest' with competitors. These are the clients who really matter.**

Customers love being listened to, so you need to go out of your way to make this possible — and be ready for some surprises.

- Birmingham Midshires Building Society carried out a customer survey which showed that interest rates came only tenth in order of importance; good service and pleasant branches were rated more highly.
- When Reebok, the sports clothing company, surveys its commercial customers it asks them to rate Reebok on issues such as 'A high quality supplier
  — has a wide range of products
  — makes deliveries at the promised time. ... etc.'
  These customers are then asked to compare Reebok against other named suppliers using the same issues.
- The Ordnance Survey has a remarkably broad customer base for its maps. "We depend upon our Consultative Committees for advice and insights. Their twice-yearly meetings ensure that carefully considered issues affecting our various markets are brought home for action. Over one hundred and forty organisations are directly represented from a spectrum spanning the Civil Aviation Authority to the National Caving Association, from the Royal Town Planning Institute to the National Farmers Union. The advent of our Consultative (Green) Papers has led to more frequent responses from these committees." (Ordnance Survey annual report).

If your customer feedback reveals that customers want a product or service which you are not currently offering, you have two clear choices: either continue not to offer it — but tell your customers why, so that they do not remain irritated by its absence — or decide that it would be a practical addition to your repertoire, in which case launch it in a way which shows its relationship to your existing range, thus capitalising on the goodwill which your customers have shown.

SUPPLIERS

For years, in comparison to sales people, buyers were the poor relation. But sectors such as motor car manufacture have demonstrated the vital contribution of suppliers to quality and the bottom line. There are two points in particular which other organisations can learn from car manufacturers.

1   The gains to be made by substantially reducing the total number of suppliers; you can then build genuine long term relationships with your selected few, take them in to your confidence and enable them to plan ahead.
2   Relationships with suppliers, although co-ordinated by the purchasing department, extend across a spectrum of your employees. Some of your front-line employees will be the prime users of suppliers' products, so why not enable them to visit the supplier and see for themselves the products being made? There are many examples of quality improvements resulting from feedback being given in this way, and it is such a missed opportunity when it does not happen. I visited a manufacturer in the Potteries, whose main suppliers were so close that you could have literally thrown a teapot out of the factory and it would have smashed on the supplier's roof. But the idea that some of the shop-floor staff should see for themselves what was happening next door had never occurred to the company.

MEDIA

Every organisation, however small, should have a clear strategy for relationships with the media: local and national newspapers; radio and television; trade journals, and so on.

Journalists cannot print what they do not know, and they are less likely to sniff out a good news story on their own initiative than one about bad news. So it should be the responsibility of some individual within your organisation to gather worthwhile items and feed them to the Press — expansion plans; export orders; staff promotions; new equipment being installed; new services launched; long service awards; individuals winning prizes or gaining qualifications; social activities; community fund raising.

You also need a system for responding to the media stories and making emergency announcements. (This is dealt with in chapter seven, *Integrated communication*.)

LOCAL GOVERNMENT

Is someone in your business responsible for liaison with the local authority? As with the media, it is best to be proactive, to get to know the key people — both council officials and elected members — so that you have built a relationship with them before you find yourself needing to deal with them in a crisis.

CENTRAL GOVERNMENT

The same applies here. Regardless of party politics, your local MP should know what your company does, your successes and what gets in the way of your growth. MPs are only too ready to pronounce about business issues but a minority has ever worked in business; so you owe it to yourself to give them first-hand understanding of it.

THE COMMUNITY

By the community we mean the people living in any area where you are a significant employer. If you are running a building society with seventeen branches, you have seventeen communities to consider.

Your legal responsibilities to these communities will have been taken care of under the local and central government headings. But the goodwill of the community towards your organisation goes beyond this. In one company a survey showed that 70% of its employees regarded the firm as very well respected in the local community, which made them proud to work for the firm. They regarded themselves as its ambassadors.

There is a real opportunity to contribute to, and gain from, voluntary organisations. Companies are in danger of taking a patronising attitude to the voluntary sector, but in my experience it has much to offer other sectors. As an example, ACENVO (Association of Chief Executives of National Voluntary Organisations) set up a working party to produce a guide on the appraisal of chief executives.* This was well ahead of most industrial and commercial companies, whose appraisal systems noticeably peter out at chief executive level.

Rather than dabbling with a large number of voluntary organisations, it is much better to select one or two and build up a relationship with them. Many companies consult their employees on the selection of the short list. One of your people — not necessarily a manager — should be the recognised co-ordinator with the voluntary sector. Sometimes there are items of equipment such as photocopiers or vehicles which you can make available. One company provides a spare office and telephone from which a voluntary service fixes transport for elderly people to hospital appointments.

Some companies second a member of staff, part-time or full time, to work with a voluntary organisation. The benefits are by no means one-way. Obviously the voluntary body welcomes the management expertise and business skills such as marketing or finance. But your secondee is likely to learn much about resilience, improvisation, and enthusiasm. As one chief executive put it, "If I could bottle the commitment which our secondee experienced at (X) (the voluntary organisation), I would give all of my staff two tablespoons each day and we would be world-class in no time."

COMPETITORS

Naturally you keep a very close eye on what your competitors are doing ... or do you? A colleague and I

*See Appendix 5

were asked by the head office of a major retailer to visit a cross-section of their branches. They are in fast-moving consumer goods, running High Street shops usually within a quarter of a mile of their competitors. It was noticeable how some of the branch managers checked the competitors' prices and displays every day, while other branches were only aware of what the competition were up to through casual comments by their customers.

I meet a wide range of Training Managers in my work, and I often ask them what methods of training their competitors are using. Overwhelmingly they know the outcomes of competitors' training in the shape of products or services — some of which have caught them on the hop. But very, very few have ever looked to see the methods of training by which their competitors give staff the skills to produce these results. There are many ways, without resorting to industrial espionage, in which you can see what training is taking place. It stands to reason that it is worth watching, because it gives you a foretaste of what is about to have an adverse affect on your business.

POTENTIAL EMPLOYEES

If our organisation's future depends primarily on the talents of its staff, how can you increase the number of candidates with the potential which you really need? Perhaps some of the most suitable potential employees do not even apply. Companies with the most effective programmes of graduate recruitment, for example, no longer dissipate their energies over fifty universities. They select a much smaller number and make sure that the company is well understood in these. This can include arranged visits, vacation work experience, and so on. An excellent vehicle is the network of Student Industrial Societies, run by undergraduates to help them select the right career.

6 overseeing the organisation

Managers and Directors

At director level, the good news is that 'managing upwards' is no longer relevant. The bad news is that a whole new element, which is best termed 'Overseeing the organisation', takes its place.

Note that the element is *not* called 'managing the organisation'. The difference between operating at management level and at board level is more than a change of job title. I interviewed Dr Brian Smith, who had been a main board director of ICI, then became chairman of Metal Box and is now chairman of BAA.

I asked him how he saw the difference between management and directorship. His reply was "I remember one of our senior managers coming in to have a strategy review and saying to him — because we were all very busy — 'I seem to have caused you an awful lot of work, and I'm sorry for that.' He said 'All you've done is make us think for the first time what we're trying to achieve rather than just managing today.' If you challenge the people at the top of a business as to what they are trying to achieve or where they are trying to go, then the thinking starts, and you can stimulate that challenge deep into the organisation."

That interview was one of nineteen with leaders of large British organisations — not just companies but schools, a national museum, and the Metropolitan Police*.

See appendix 5

A fascinating pattern emerged from these leaders'
descriptions of the most important influences on their
effectiveness at different stages of their careers.
We called these stages:

the hill   When they were just starting their
climb up the steep hill of management
experience;

the high ground   When they took up a general
management post, and finally left
behind their original specialism;

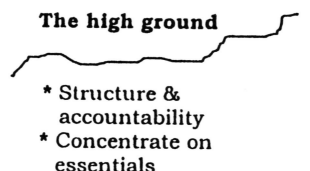

the horizon
The view from the top, at the very zenith of the organisation.

The horizon

* **Long term vision**
* **Face to face contact with staff**
* **Trust managers - give them headroom**

When climbing the hill, what most helped their development was a series of challenges, put in perspective by a mentor.

Reaching the high ground, their priorities were to clarify structure and the accountability of individuals. They also had to become very disciplined at concentrating on essential issues: general managers have to make unpopular decisions between several claims on scarce resources. At the very top, 'the horizon', they articulated a long term vision but balanced this by maintaining sufficient face-to-face contact with staff, in order to be in touch with reality. But they were careful not to get in the way of managers, who need headroom (see page 63, A sense of identity).

Mentoring

One of the implications of this analysis is the importance of mentoring. Although mentoring is most commonly offered to graduate trainees, it need not be limited to them, nor need the mentor necessarily be a very senior person. What matters most is the right 'chemistry' between mentor and learner.

A mentor's main role is to help the learner achieve a sense of perspective. A mentor should emphatically *not* try to give the learner unfair advantages such as accelerated promotion: for this reason the term 'learner' is preferable to 'protégé.' Although a mentor's repertoire of skills will include coaching, the two processes are different. The distinctive contributions of mentor and coach are as follows:

	Mentor	Coach
Relationship to learner	Private, individual	Private or public; individual or group
Relationship to learner's manager	Your line manager must not be your mentor	Line manager can be coach
Contact with learner	Intermittent, medium to long term	Can be very short term
Main agenda	Context within which learner's work is done	Content of learner's work
Proximity	Need not always involve face to face contact, e.g. can be through correspondence or telephone calls	Difficult to achieve without face to face contact
Outcomes	Long term career development	Short to medium term improved performance.

There is no reason why directors should not have mentors — or for that matter, coaches. Their need to learn and to hone their skills does not diminish on promotion to the board. Indeed, arguably their responsibility as role models for continuing personal development increases commensurately with their seniority.

The 'added value' approach becomes more and more important, the higher up the organisation you move. A headteacher described it like this: "I am delivering my added value when my energy is spent prioritising ideas which come from below rather than pushing from above". If you become a director, your colleagues will look to you for a strategic view of your function — marketing, or finance, etc. But the professional expertise in your function rests within your specialist team.

I saw an excellent demonstration of this when I attended an annual general meeting of the National Trust. These AGMs, unlike those of most companies, are pretty lively, with members sounding off about foxhunting, coastal pollution and so on. Angus Stirling, the Trust's director-general, handled the meeting in masterly fashion. As each question was raised by the members, he would say "Our finance director is the expert on that — I will ask him to answer" or "Let me introduce our South West region controller — he is very knowledgeable on this", etc. But Angus Stirling answered the most difficult or contentious questions himself. Here was a leader giving public acknowledgement to the strength of his team, but also not shirking his personal accountability.

Your value to the board comes from your broad experience, your judgement, your personality. Really impressive boards work as genuine teams. I talked with the personnel director of a food company, who was going to be away at the time of the board meeting the following week. But he was quite relaxed about it: "Any of my colleagues can take the necessary personnel decisions — we are an interchangeable team". A starstruck interviewer once asked Sir John Harvey-Jones how he coped with "the huge responsibility of running ICI" when he was its chairman. Harvey-Jones put him right by pointing out that he had hundreds of managers whose job it was to run ICI. "My sole job as chairman is to run the board. If I do that well, everything flows from it".

This also represents the death-knell of traditional succession planning. That usually involved elaborate plans for James B to succeed George R as marketing manager in three years time, having meanwhile been seconded to X and led a project on Y. When you reviewed these plans three years later, many had not actually happened because unexpected events had stopped them.

But the more basic flaw in such plans was that they assumed that the job which George R. had been carrying out would continue to be needed once George disappeared for whatever reason.

A much healthier approach is what might be called zero-based organisation development. Look at each job which currently exists and analyse it *twice*:

1   What added value is produced by the job itself (regardless of the job holder)? In the above example, do you necessarily need a marketing manager as such? Is it a core activity, or could it be outsourced? Is the post at the right level in the organisation? Does it overlap with other positions — laterally or vertically? In the words of the music-hall ballad, "Would it be missed if it didn't exist?"
2   Analysis also reveals what is contributed by the particular individual in the post at present: his personal added value. What is George R's distinctive style? What special skills does he bring to the role? What does he offer beyond the confines of the post itself? Put starkly, what will his obituary say about him?

More often than not when you subject a post to this double scrutiny it becomes clear that far from looking for a clone of George R, you should be changing the whole shape of the job when he moves on (if not before!) — double the job, or halve it, or hive off this part to someone else, eliminate it, or let George R write his own job description to optimise his contribution. Now more than ever, structures should be organic: let us not stifle talent for the sake of a neat organisation chart.

The Board's collective added value

If a Board is not working well it often turns out to be because its members have not properly worked out the special role of the Board. We are back with added value again, but this time in a collective rather than an individual version.

Working with boards, I find two approaches help them to clarify their added value. The first is to consider the words *distinctive* and *fundamental*. You are on the board of a food company which started eighty years ago as a family business. What should be retained as the best of its traditions? How can you retain customer goodwill as the business ceases to be family controlled? What sets your firm apart from its rivals? What is unusual, different, *distinctive* about it?

The Board should add value by identifying the organisation's distinctive features. As the most senior people, they are best placed to do this. But paradoxically, the organisation's newest recruits (at all levels) also have an important contribution to make here. Because they have only just joined, they have a fresh perspective.

At The Industrial Society, we run regular induction courses at which all employees who have recently joined come together for a day, regardless of their location or position. As Human Resources Director I run a session on the course during which I ask them two questions which never fail to produce information of real value. These are:

- **What is distinctive about this organisation? (What is different from companies where you have previously worked? What is unusual or special?**
- **What could we do better? (As a newcomer, what do you find unhelpful/cumbersome/difficult to understand/outdated/etc.?)**

I regularly report back to my fellow-directors the trends emerging from the replies to these two questions. Some trends are very encouraging; any which are not lead to an improvement in our procedures.

Then there is the question about what is *fundamental* to the organisation. What would you go to the barricades about? What are your core values? Sometimes these issues are so much in the bloodstream of the organisation that they have never been made explicit. Whether you choose to express them in a mission, vision or values statement is entirely up to you. The important point is that you should check for a common understanding of these fundamentals. This is not brainwashing. If approached in the right way it can genuinely strengthen people's pride in the organisation.

The second approach is a development from the three circles of action-centred leadership (ACL). ACL is designed for individuals, but it can easily be adapted for the corporate level:

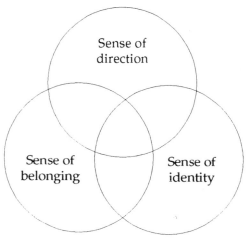

The diagram shows what the board has to provide to the organisation, no matter whether it has twenty employees or twenty thousand.

- **A SENSE OF DIRECTION** — deciding its long term aims, its broad plans beyond the immediate future; and when from time to time the strategy changes, communicating the *Why* as well as the *what* (see page 11).
- **A SENSE OF BELONGING** — creating a climate in which the various operating units see benefit from being part of a larger whole. For example in a group of companies, the board may set down financial principles under which operating businesses can obtain finance for development

from the corporate centre, and so on. Another example comes from the National Museums and Galleries on Merseyside, a group of eight establishments which all ultimately report to a single board of trustees.

The sense of belonging which each museum or gallery perceives arises amongst other things from their ability to promote each other. If they can individually attract visitors to Merseyside, all eight establishments potentially benefit: so they co-ordinate their marketing and publicity programmes.

A SENSE OF IDENTITY — the corollary of a sense of belonging. Togetherness must not become stifling. To take the museums and galleries example, the director of an art gallery would not take kindly to a member of the corporate board telling him how to hang his pictures. Individuals must be allowed to do things their own way as much as possible.

Walking the job

Walking the job is one way through which a director or senior manager can convey a sense of direction, belonging and identity. Walking round your organisation and talking informally with employees at their workplace is not a casual stroll. It should be purposeful without being contrived and stuffy. Directors who do it well find these 'do's and don'ts' useful:

Do   Ask people about facts *and* feelings. Ask them to explain what they are doing and where it fits; and how they feel about changes, the organisation's prospects, etc.

Do   Set a good example over safety. (Some directors have been known to decline to wear safety goggles or a hard hat).

Do   Listen, and show that you are listening.

Do   Look closely at notice boards and test them against the checklist in Appendix 3.

Do   Go out of your way to encourage and praise.

Do   use walking the job to build people's confidence. A factory manager in GKN, with 200 employees, used to find that by the end of a morning walking the job "I had acquired 200 new problems to solve." He learnt to empower his people to decide for themselves.

Don't Assume that everyone knows who you are. Introduce yourself by name and position to each person you talk to.

Don't Make policy commitments 'on the hoof'. (You will inevitably be 'lobbied' by some of the people you talk to.) Instead, arrange for the response to their problem or suggestion to be delivered back to them by their own manager.

Don't Undercut the local manager's authority. If you see or hear things which are clearly wrong, discuss them with the manager privately.

Don't Bluff. If you are asked for a comment on some work procedure which you are not familiar with, use this as an opportunity to learn (if it is not trivial) or refer the person to their own manager or relevant specialist.

Don't Adopt a false bonhomie with people whom you hardly know. They will see through this straight away.

If you are responsible for several widely-spread locations, you may want your 'walking the job' to take a different form. I interviewed a senior civil servant in the Ministry of Defence in London. He was responsible for MoD units all over the UK, and the system which he had evolved was as follows. He would contact the head of an

MoD establishment (a research centre, or a dockyard, and so on) a few weeks ahead and arrange a convenient date for a visit. He would ask the head of the establishment to fix two presentations to him for that occasion: the first on a subject which he (the London civil servant) wanted to hear about — perhaps progress on a research topic, or comments on a new way of working in the dockyard — and the second on a subject of the local staff's own choice: maybe something they were proud of, or worried about, or whatever.

He also requested that the staff making these presentations should not consist only of managers, but be a reasonable cross-section.

What a good model for a two-way communication flow!

Finally, when walking the job, pride comes before a fall. Victor Watson told this story against himself: he was chairman of Waddingtons (the company which makes the 'Monopoly' board game) and also president of the Printers' Charitable Corporation (PCC). "On a visit to the PCC home in Bletchley I met a lady who was pushing a zimmer frame. Doing my bit as PCC president, I said to her 'Do you know who I am?' She replied 'Ask matron — she'll know'."

7 integrated communication

5-way management is a natural tool for producing a truly integrated communication system. When my colleagues in The Industrial Society's surveys and audits unit carry out employee surveys in organisations, they typically find a whole range of communications systems in use (see box below).

There is nothing wrong with using a wide variety of communication methods: quite the contrary. But they must be integrated, not piecemeal, if their impact is not to be jeopardised.

Communication methods — examples	
Face to face:	**Written**
Meetings	Notice boards
Roadshows	Memos
1:1 sessions	Annual reports
Team briefings	Suggestion schemes
Consultative committees	Newsletters
Trade union representatives	House magazine
Focus groups	Attitude surveys
The grapevine	Questionnaires
Quality circles	Management bulletins
Walking the job	Displays & exhibitions
Annual conferences	Briefing packs
Open days	Handbooks, manuals
'Speak up' systems	

Using technology:	
E-mail	
Videos	
Telephone	
Voice mail	
Video conferencing	
Hotlines	

Untold millions of pounds are spent each year by employers endeavouring to communicate with their employees. Much of this is wasted by failing to integrate the methods used into a coherent whole. A survey of 915 British organisations* showed that:

- **Nearly three quarters have no written policy on communications**
- **Only one in three link employee communications to the business plan**
- **Only one in ten try to measure the cost of communications**
- **Only one manager in four has received any training in an overall understanding of communications systems**

In an integrated communications structure you have clear policies for communicating downwards, upwards, across the organisation and externally. The fifth element in 5-way management, managing yourself, is represented by a person or a small team accountable for developing and maintaining the communications structure and assessing its effectiveness. In a small organisation this will not need to be a full time role or anything approaching it; but the essential point is that someone is seen to be the co-ordinator.

Using the above approach, you can establish

*Employee Communications, Managing Best Practice no.1, The Industrial Society 1994 objectives for each of the four directions, and then make intelligent choices of appropriate methods. Some of the principles which may find their way into your objectives are these:

- **Consistency** is vital. Employees should be confident that they will hear the same message through several sources. If I read a notice signed by the chief executive and understand it to say X, then my manager talks to me on the same subject and it sounds more like 70% X plus 30% Y, which version should I believe?
- Good communication is **two-way**. It is not enough to convey a message: you have to check that it has been correctly received. Therefore feedback systems are crucial.
- **Speed** matters. It is tempting to wait until every part of an issue has been clarified before saying anything; but if you do, the vacuum will be filled by rumours and you then have to demolish them before putting the true version in their stead. A good rubric is "In times of change, communicate little and often".
- "**Actions** speak louder than words, and actions by top management scream" (John Humble). Sophisticated presentations can be rendered worthless in a flash if managers' actions do not support their messages.
- You will never kill the **grapevine** — indeed it is arguably a healthy safety valve. But you rely on it at your peril. A good grapevine has an uncanny ability to forecast decisions accurately even before they have been made — but it then twists the motive behind the decision into the most cynical shape.
- Effective communication balances **what, why and how,** (see page 26).

    Using these principles, you can draft your communication objectives. A skeleton might include the points listed below; much of course depends on the size and shape of your organisation and especially on how many locations it includes.

Communicating downwards

Objectives:

- To ensure that every employee receives *regular* information which enables him to understand his part in the organisation. This will include progress reports on the organisation as a whole in broad terms, but more detail about the progress of his own department or unit.
- To enable the leader of each team at every level to put across information to the team face to face in order to achieve commitment, gauge understanding and deal with questions.
- To have a system capable of conveying urgent information very rapidly to every person who needs it.
- To build employees' confidence in the organisation by ensuring that when speculative or inaccurate stories about the organisation are put across in the media (e.g. television, local newspapers, etc.), a reliable statement by the company will follow rapidly.
- To ensure that credit is given where it is due; e.g. appropriate prominence in annual reports etc. to 'backroom' employees instead of endless photographs of the directors.
- To make it clear that employee representatives are not expected to carry out managers' responsibility for downwards communication.

Communicating upwards

Objectives:

- To create a blame-free culture in which employees' ideas, worries, concerns and questions are relayed upwards without being diluted. ('Don't shoot the messenger').
- To respect the role of employee representatives by giving them training in how to carry out their role effectively, by genuinely consulting them (i.e. not just

trimming the edges of decisions) and by giving them access to senior managers.

- By requiring managers to report on reactions by their teams to downward messages, and by providing answers to questions raised within a short timescale.

Communicating across the organisation

Objectives:
- To build and exploit the organisation's knowledge base by appropriate sharing of information — especially to avoid duplication of work.
- To provide a means of avoiding misunderstandings or the inadvertent lack of consideration of the impact of a decision on another part of the company.
- To achieve synergy by 'the left hand knowing what the right hand is doing'.
- To give the best possible service to *external* customers/clients by achieving *internal* co-ordination.

Communicating externally

Objectives:
- To provide a speedy, unbureaucratic system for customers/clients to obtain answers to questions or redress for mistakes.
- To promote our products and services honestly and vigorously to our market.
- To encourage external contacts of all kinds to provide feedback to us on our strengths and weaknesses as an organisation.
- To respond promptly and accurately to request for information from regulators, central and local government, the media and other relevant organisations.
- To come across to potential recruits as a responsible employer — a good place to work.

*   *   *

Once you have discussed and written down objectives such as these, you can plan your communications strategy — how to select the right method(s) for each objective.

Communication methods — strengths and limitations

It is helpful to bear in mind some general points about the strengths and limitations of the three main themes of communication — verbal, written, and technological.

VERBAL METHODS (e.g. meetings, briefing, walking the job, etc.)

Strengths:
- The communicator's commitment can be conveyed
- Immediate feedback e.g. in the form of questions
- Opportunity for many people to contribute
- Preparation time can be very short in some cases

Limitations:
- Relies on personality of the communicator
- Can be expensive, e.g. the 'opportunity costs' of those involved in a sizeable meeting
- In a meeting covering several topics, not everything will be relevant to everyone present
- Absentees may be forgotten or inadequately followed up
- A written record may still be required (e.g. minutes of a meeting)

WRITTEN METHODS (e.g. memos, notices, newsletters, etc.)

Strengths:
- Consistency of the message can be achieved (NB this means consistency in what the written words say, not necessarily in how they are understood by the receivers)

- Precision can be achieved through careful wording
- Illustrations can significantly enhance understanding
- Provides a permanent record

Limitations:
- No feedback — you cannot ask a notice board a question
- Less easy to convey commitment and enthusiasm in writing than in person
- Can involve substantial preparation time e.g. redrafting
- People often react against sheer volume of written material, and may not give it the attention it deserves

METHODS USING TECHNOLOGY (e.g. E-mail, videos, telephone)

Strengths:
- Speed — a telephone call can be immediate
- Cost effective — no need to travel to a meeting
- Telephone allows immediate feedback

Limitations:
- Equipment subject to breakdown
- Cost: videos can be very expensive to make
- Except for telephone, no guarantee that the message has been received
- A written record may still be required

Appropriate methods

Looking through the list of objectives under the four headings (see page 69), there are some points to consider.

COMMUNICATING DOWNWARDS

- The three circles are useful. Are you communicating a sense of direction — e.g. by regular progress reports on the organisation as a whole? — A sense of belonging — by news of those parts of the organisation with which your team have the closest contact? — A sense of identity — by the progress of your own unit and the contribution to it of each individual?

- Team briefing is a very well-tried and effective method of doing this, especially as it entails the personal involvement of the leader of each team at every level.
- A proper team briefing system covers every individual and includes provision for absentees; so a special, urgent brief can be conveyed in an emergency situation.
- There is no way you can prevent the media publishing speculative stories about your organisation — and sometimes these will prove correct. The important point is to build your employees' confidence by providing a vigorous and speedy rebuttal if a Press report is false, or coolly ignoring a story which is not worth bothering about. What you must avoid is your own staff beginning to rely on the media for accurate news about your company before they have been informed through your own channels. One example was when production workers in a cosmetics company saw, on their own television screens at home one evening, a TV commercial for a new product which they had made — before they had been informed of its launch onto the market.
- It is only too easy for an organisation's annual report to become completely off-balance. It features highlights of the directors' careers; shows them shaking hands with various VIPs; and apart from the usual platitudes about employees as the company's greatest asset, pictures and text about individual employees are missing. This is a wasted opportunity which can cause deep resentment.
- Employee representatives can find themselves in a 'no-win' situation if they have to fill downwards communications vacuums caused by inadequate management. They become regarded as 'management mouthpieces' when their main role is to communicate upwards. So make sure that this does not happen.
- You are required by law to display various notices (e.g. health and safety). The general standard of most company noticeboards is very low and their potential

as part of an integrated communications system is not exploited. By following the checklist in Appendix 4 you can markedly improve the impact of your notices.

COMMUNICATING UPWARDS

Several steps can be taken to promote a blame free culture, including:

- Converting many policies, which are prescriptive, into guidelines, which set out several options. This gives people more scope to use their initiative; it also gives more power to those policies which need to remain rigid.
- 'Accentuate the positive' — for example when managers walk the job, they should seek out examples of things going well.
- Praise and recognition — e.g. praise in writing (see page 00)
- Carry out 'post mortems' on successes achieved as well as on failures. If a project was completed on time and within budget, examine how it was done so that the success can be cloned.
- If you want employee representatives to play a full and constructive part in the organisation, they must be completely clear about their role. They may well need training in interpersonal skills, meetings procedure, report writing, and so on. Above all, they should be genuinely consulted — this means giving them enough time to discuss issues at the formative stage with their colleagues. One way of making consultative committees more effective is to map out a series of topics which will be discussed over the next few months, so that people have adequate advance notice and can consider them thoroughly, instead of being bounced into off-the-cuff comments during a meeting.
- Team briefing can be very effective as a 'downward' system; but its impact is diluted if it does not entail clear feedback upwards of reactions to the message. All briefers should be required to report feedback very rapidly (e.g. within 48 hours of the briefing session) and to obtain authoritative answers to queries raised.

COMMUNICATION ACROSS THE ORGANISATION

- The objectives/support grid (see page 00) is very useful as a method of sharing information laterally. Other methods include learning resource centres and a directory of 'who does what' within the organisation; the latter must be regularly updated.
- The difficulty about 'left hand/right hand' is that 'You don't know what you don't know'. That is, you may not realise the value of receiving some piece of information until it is actually presented to you. It is easy to go into overdrive in an effort to rectify this, and to create streams of circulars and creeping algae of committees which tell everybody about everything. A far more realistic approach is to establish low-key informal, temporary contacts through which colleagues find out more about each other's activities. If these contacts prove fruitful, ways will emerge naturally in which the right information is shared. Very often the most useful exchanges are about issues in the pipeline rather than those already in full flow.
- We have to remember that external customers or clients are not interested in our internal bureaucracy. The worst scenario is when an external customer cannot obtain a straight answer to a simple question, or redress for a straightforward mistake, without having to complete an obstacle course of excuses and 'It's not this department, you'll have to call head office.' Procedures should be designed from the customer's viewpoint — which always means maximum simplicity and a willingness by every employee to see that the customer is satisfied, even though the initial query may have started with the wrong person.

COMMUNICATING EXTERNALLY

- If we were able to keep a tally of the number of encounters in a year between our own employees (at all levels) and outsiders, the total would probably astonish us. We can use a proportion of these encounters to provide invaluable feedback — and what is more, it can be done very cost-effectively.

- One organisation which runs leisure centres uses its car park supervisors to ask customers some quick and simple questions as they return to their cars after using the facilities. And every visitor to Trifast in Sussex is asked to complete a short questionnaire in reception before they leave, which invites them to make one improvement suggestion based on their visit.

- The importance of realism in recruitment advertising is best demonstrated by the experience of some multinational companies trying to attract graduates. Those which have done best over the medium term — i.e. not only recruiting but retaining high performers — have gradually realised the power of using recent recruits themselves to tell their stories, warts and all.

8 360° appraisal

It is easy to caricature the worst kind of conventional appraisal scheme; a monologue from your immediate manager, looking only into the past and flushing out all the minor mistakes which you thought had been long forgotten, and with little concern for your development. In one company the appraisal scheme only involved the individual and the immediate manager, and had effectively become an annual form-filling chore. A manager and secretary had worked together for eleven years and when the dreaded appraisal form came round for the eleventh time, the manager had run out of anything new to say, so he simply wrote across the form 'Mrs Evans is coming along nicely'!

The long-overdue backlash against these fruitless charades has come in recent years first in the shape of upwards appraisal (where the views of your direct reports are sought) and then in the more adventurous all-round version most often known as 360°. The 3M Company use an alternative term, 'multi-source feedback'.

It is immediately apparent that 5-way management suits this approach admirably. There are very many versions, so let us look at the more common ones.

HOW DO YOU CHANGE TO A 360° APPRAISAL SCHEME?

There is a strong consensus amongst those organisations which are using the scheme that you should move steadily and not rush. As examples, PowerGen used a pilot scheme; 3M tried it first in small groups; Rover moved through three stages — first, self assessment; next, appraisal by colleagues and immediate manager; third, direct reports were added.

WHY USE 360° APPRAISAL?

Amongst the reasons put forward by organisations are these:

- If your appraisal only involves your M1 and M2 (i.e. managing upwards), it is limited to your own function and ignores internal customers.
- Flatter structures have accentuated lateral communication, so the comments of your peers are relevant (i.e. managing across the organisation)
- If you are in charge of a team, it is legitimate to collect their views on what is most and least helpful in the way you lead them (managing downwards).
- Organisations exist to satisfy customers or clients, so we should tap their comments on your effectiveness (managing outwards).

In addition to these, the three main reasons emerging from a survey* of 237 companies using 360° were:

- To improve individual performance
- To fit in with a more empowered culture
- To improve corporate performance

WHO SUPPLIES THE COMMENTS?

People from whom feedback can be sought can include any or all of the following:

- Your M1
- Your M2
- Other managers at M1 level
- Colleagues at your own level (peer appraisal)
- Your direct reports
- People within the organisation with whom you have worked closely during the year — these people may not necessarily be at your own level. The most typical category would be fellow members of a project team, who could be from various levels and departments.

*360° appraisal (Managing Best Practice no.17, The Industrial Society 1995)

- Customers
- Suppliers
- Regulators, auditors

From the length of this list you can quickly understand why organisations advise moving steadily. If all employees in your organisation were appraised by all of the above groups you would be creating a blizzard of paper.

WHAT ARE THE COMMENTS BASED ON?
The most common approach is to use a list of competencies which have been identified as significant for your organisation. Mercury One2One, for instance, uses twenty competencies, called personal success factors, which fall under five main headings:

- understanding what needs to be done
- building a winning team
- managing yourself
- working with others
- focus on results

(Note the relevance of 5-way management to these headings).

HOW ARE THE COMMENTS GATHERED AND TRANSMITTED?
Here there are many variations. The most usual way of gathering the comments is by questionnaires; other versions include an open meeting with the person being appraised, chaired by an independent person such as an external consultant. Once the comments have been gathered, it is common for them to be summarised by an HR specialist and then presented to the person being appraised in a confidential interview with his M1.

HOW SHOULD PEOPLE PREPARE TO TAKE PART IN 360° APPRAISAL?
Experience shows that many people who are about to be appraised in this way for the first time feel nervous,

dreading that the outcome will be a demoralising catalogue of their faults. But in practice the great majority of 'recipients' find the process very helpful, particularly if the comments focus on their development needs.

The other point which has also emerged strongly is that the 'providers' of comments can feel equally nervous — especially if the comments are about someone senior to themselves. So before embarking on 360° appraisal, a short training session (typically half a day) is very worthwhile. This should cover the process from the viewpoint both of recipient and of provider; and there should be additional guidance for managers who will find themselves the final link in the chain, charged with conveying the gist of other people's comments in a constructive fashion.

SUMMARY ON 360° APPRAISAL

There seems little doubt that the 360° method will grow: over a third of respondents to the survey felt that 360° would be the most popular system eight years from now. The organisational climate must be right and the system should be introduced steadily and with care, keeping the tone constructive throughout. If you are already using 5-way management in your daily operations, you will be particularly well placed to benefit from 360°. For an in-depth review on the process and practical applications of 360° Appraisal, a book on the subject is available from the Industrial Society. (See Resource List.)

360° AND YOUR ADDED VALUE

As you have defined your own added value (see chapter 2, Managing Yourself), each annual 360° appraisal will provide the ideal check on how closely you are matching your added value in practice.

Rate yourself, and through the 360° method involve others in rating your ability to discharge these core functions. Any aspects where you fall short can be tackled in one of four ways:

- improve your ability, e.g. be being coached, going on a training course, understudying an expert, etc.
- delegate that aspect to one of your team, or in discussion with your manager transfer it to a colleague who is better able to handle it
- sub-contract it, e.g. if it really does not matter whether that aspect is carried out within the organisation or outside, it may be more economical to use an external specialist to do it for you
- question whether it actually needs to be done at all. If no one did it, who would suffer? Has it outlived its usefulness?

9 summary

5-way management provides a framework for effectiveness. You may have realised that your work is off-balance: you are spending an undue amount of time on one element at the expense of others. When you move into a new role you can use 5-way management to check where your attention should best be directed.

You can use it as the basis of appraising performance, whether in the traditional way or in a 360° version. It can be the basis for job descriptions and succession plans.

At the corporate level there is a desperate need to make communication more integrated, by using one method to reinforce another, and I trust that you see its contribution in this area.

I hope that the examples given in the book will encourage you to put it to good use.

10 appendices

APPENDIX I MANAGING UPWARDS

How to Manage Your Boss

By Marie Mosely

Whatever type of boss you have, these strategies will help you get the boss off your back and on your side.

1 **Be pro-active**. Initiate good ideas to help your boss, the team and the organisation.
2 **Manage change**. Don't be fazed by it — changes offer opportunities. If your office or job is being redefined, be the first to identify what you can do that's useful and exciting.
3 **Understand the differences between you and the boss**. Don't think you're damned because you're opposites. Identify the differences and work out how they can complement each other. If you're a natural teambuilder and they're a doer, you may make the perfect team.
4 **Agree the levels of performance with your boss**. Evaluate and review your performance regularly with your boss so you both know you're on the right track.
5 **Let your boss know your intentions for the future**. Where do you want to be in two to five years' time? How can you and the boss work on a development plan to enable you to achieve your goals?

The chart on the next page shows how to manage bosses of four types: doer, carer, thinker and teambuilder.

(For more information, contact Marie Mosely, business psychologist (01202) 896037)

How to Manage Your Boss

	DOER	CARER	THINKER	TEAMBUILDER
What are they like	Doers love to organise and be in charge. They are competitive, enjoy taking risks and relish challenges. A high quality Doer is a joy to work for - you know where you stand and what's expected of you. A 'low quality' Doer will not listen and will try to 'railroad' decisions	Carers listen. They are accessible, loyal and supportive. They want people to feel good about themselves. A good Carer manages by empowerment. A low quality Carer worries because they are too sensitive to the needs of others, so they make no decisions at all.	Thinkers enjoy analysis, research and planning. Thinkers tend to work on their own. They are self-reliant and usually fair. The high quality Thinker lets you get on with your job. The low quality Thinker has an aversion to risk taking which can make them overly nit-picking	Teambuilders are at their best when they manage by consensus. A high quality Teambuilder includes staff in decision-making and values a harmonious team atmosphere. Poor quality Teambuilders spend so much time looking at options they never make a decision.
They want you to	• take responsibility • be flexible • show you have confidence in them • communicate your messages briefly	• be accessible • care about others • be loyal • be supportive to them and the team • give of your time	• research your ideas well • be self-reliant • provide detail • be consistent	• be open and flexible • work for the team, not yourself • contribute your ideas • be friendly and sociable
They don't want you to	• need instructing • question their authority • give them too much detail • waste their time	• be unkind or rude • be a bad listener • be so task-focused that you forget the 'people' aspect • be too competitive	• take risks • interrupt them • need a lot of their time • be too flexible • be emotional	• be rigid in your thinking • keep ideas to yourself • be too quick to make decisions • be too task-focused

APPENDIX II MANAGING DOWNWARDS

Front line experience for Employment Service senior managers

Regular clients visiting Barnsbury (Kings Cross) Jobcentre in London, during a week in May could have been forgiven for thinking they had gone to the wrong office. Where were all the familiar faces? Had the office had a complete change of staff over the weekend? Yes, it had! For a full week, the office was run by 70 senior Employment Service managers from London and South East Regional Office.

Basis for sensible decisions

Richard Foster, the Regional Director, explained why they were doing it. "We need senior managers who really understand the nuts and bolts. This week will help us get a better understanding of clients' needs and the problems our local office teams face. It will give us a better basis for making sensible decisions in the future. It's also a significant team building exercise for managers in our new structure."

A small team of 16 permanent Barnsbury people — dubbed the 'safety net' — stood by while everyone else took the opportunity to take a week's training — a combination of individually selected courses and a team event to plan for future reorganisation in the office.

Countdown

A great deal of planning, spanning more than six months, went into the project. Managers received special training and carried out familiarisation visits to the Jobcentre.

Senior management's views on their new jobs

Jenny Eastabrook, Assistant Regional Director, spent the week as a payments administrative officer: "I've enjoyed being out on reception and the front line dealing with clients. The work is totally different from my usual job but there are still pressures. For example you're constantly having to make judgements about when you can help and when to refer enquiries to someone else, to avoid wasting the client's and your own time."

Jenny said she would be returning to regional office with "a powerful message on the amount of paperwork."

Chris Nicol, a Senior Business Manager, commented that his week on the benefits sections "has really brought home how difficult and tiring the job can be."

Lessons learnt

Some other messages which came through were:

"Why does every office do this differently?"
"It's made me more aware of unforeseen problems."
"As a result of this exercise" said the Regional Director, "a wide range of changes are to be introduced to help local offices run better — e.g. less paper, IT improvements, better queue management and improved manager training. More generally, it has made us realise the vital importance of senior managers getting to grips with the detail of how key processes operate." He added: "The agency has learned a great deal and it has been tremendous for staff morale. Front line staff now know that their managers too know what it's like 'at the sharp end'. It has involved a lot of hard work, but we are now beginning to reap the benefits. I would recommend managers in any organisation to try it themselves."

Adapted from an article in 'Management Matters', produced by the Cabinet Office, with acknowledgement to Sue Lilley and Liz Friend.

APPENDIX III MANAGING OUTWARDS

Careers Guidance in Hampshire

Hampshire Guidance & Careers Service originally drew up this grid to co-ordinate all careers activities within the county. The service is now provided by VT Southern Careers Ltd.

The full grid extends to an A3 page and shows in the left hand column the entitlements and across the top the various partners who have a role to play. Only part of the grid is illustrated here (the two remaining entitlements, not shown, are 'experience of work' and 'recording achievement and planning for the future'; the eight remaining partners, not shown, are the TEC, local education authority, education-business partnership, governors, teachers, VT Southern Careers, Young People, and other partners). Equal opportunities permeate all five entitlements.

The grid achieves two results: all partners are clear about their own contribution to the various objectives, and the left hand knows what the right is doing because the whole grid is seen by all concerned. It is a very practical version of the objective/support grid described in chapter 4.

	Partner's potential contribution		
Entitlement	Schools and Colleges	Employers	Parents
A planned programme of careers education	written documentation agreed delivery model identified staff to manage and deliver resourcing	involvement in curriculum projects providing employer expertise	need opportunities to sample and understand the programme
Access to information	accessible and coordinated information materials IT resources, access and maintenance information handling skills	employer and trade information recruitment literature sponsorship and personnel for conventions etc.	PTA fund-raising parents as AOTs (Auxiliary Outplacement Teacher) and role models influencing students to use information
Access to individual guidance	integrated approach to guidance provide student information trained staff agreement with VTSC for guidance	information on employer perspective training in interview skills practice interviews	recognition of input by parents and involvement in the process (e.g.) attendance at interviews

APPENDIX IV INTEGRATED COMMUNICATION

Notice Boards — checklist

- Ensure that you display appropriate statutory regulations e.g. health and safety, etc.
- Display notices on similar topics together, e.g. a section for promotions, transfers etc.; for committees; for policy matters; for social events.
- Each notice should have a 'remove by' date. Each notice board should be updated daily.
- The best way of keeping notice boards tidy and smart is to have a named person accountable for each board. His or her name can be shown on the board so that people are aware of whom to contact.
- Make clear who is allowed to display notices. The simplest system may be to channel everything through the person accountable for each board.
- Assume that every board will be seen by visitors as well as by your own staff, so take care over confidential or commercially sensitive information.
- Urgent notices should be marked in some way. Their impact is lessened if they are displayed for too long.
- Every notice should include the name of its author so that any comments or feedback go to the right person.
- Take a strong line over graffiti. Not every notice will contain welcome information, but honest efforts to communicate deserve respect.
- Review the position of all notice boards once a year. Changes in site layout may leave some boards in the wrong places. Check that they are legible by people with disabilities.
- A notice is not normally the best way to convey 'pep talks' or general reprimands, because a notice lacks person-to-person contact. In addition, as visitors are likely to see such notices they may spread a bad image for your organisation.
- Set basic standards for the physical appearance of notices: grubby hand-written notices, or those

produced on ancient typewriters, should not be accepted. If your organisation has a "house style" for documents, this should apply to notices.

- Use notice boards as part of an integrated communications programme which includes face-to-face briefings, consultation, bulletins, etc. If you have sufficient IT capacity, E-mail provides an additional method to supplement paper notices.

resource list

MANAGING YOURSELF

Debra Allcock	*Time and Workload Management*	
	The Industrial Society,	ISBN 1 85835 154 5
Paddy O'Brien	*Assertiveness: a Working Guide*	
	The Industrial Society &	
	Nicholas Brealey Publishing	ISBN 1 85788 1012
Andrew Forrest	*50 ways to personal development*	
	The Industrial Society	ISBN 185835 239 8

MANAGING UPWARDS

Jonathan Coates	*Managing Upwards*	
	Gower 1994,	ISBN 0 566 07485 0
John Crawley	*Constructive Conflict Management*	
	(see chapter, "A conflict with the boss")	
	Nicholas Brealey Publishing	ISBN 1 85788
Derek Rowntree	*How to Manage Your Boss*	
	Sphere Books	ISBN 0 7474 0052 0

MANAGING DOWNWARDS

Video	*Talking to the Team*	
	The Industrial Society and Video Arts	
John Whitmore	*Coaching for Performance*	
	Nicholas Brealey Publishing	ISBN 1 85788 013)

MANAGING ACROSS

Video	*Good Vibrations* (interpersonal skills)
	The Industrial Society

MANAGING OUTWARDS

The Industrial Society	*Customer Care*	
	Managing Best Practice No 9, 1995	ISBN 1355 1515 09
Video	*Negotiating for a Positive Outcome*	
	Tarragon	
Alan Fowler	*Negotiating Skills & Strategies*	ISBN 0 85292 664 2
	IPD (2nd edition)	

OVERSEEING THE ORGANISATION

Andrew Forrest	*Leaders — the learning curve of achievement*	
& Patrick Tolfree	The Industrial Society	
	(interviews with 19 British leaders)	ISBN 0 85290 906 3
Bob Garratt	*The Fish Rots From the Head*	
	Harper Collins Business	ISBN 0 00 255613 8

ACENVO   Appraising the chief
                                executive: a guide   ISBN 1 900685 01 9

INTEGRATED COMMUNICATION
The Industrial Society   *Upward Communication*
                                Managing Best Practice
                                No 15, 1995   ISBN 1 85855 021 X
John Lidstone   *Face the Press*
                                The Industrial Society &
                                Nicholas Brealey Publishing   ISBN 1 85788 005 6
Linda Fairbrother   *Your message and the Media*
                                The Industrial Society &
                                Nicholas Brealey Publishing   ISBN 1 85788 006 4
Liz Cochrane   *Influencing Communication*
                                The Industrial Society   ISBN 1 85835 488 9
The Industrial Society   Employee Communication
                                An Integrated Approach   ISBN 1 85835 819 1

360° APPRAISAL
Laurence Handy   *360° Feedback: unguided missile or powerful weapon?*
                                Ashridge Management College
Steve France   *360° Appraisal*
                                The Industrial Society   ISBN 1 85835 478 1